SPEAK OUT.

IT'S THE LANGUAGE OF SUCCESS.

Do you have a cause to promote, an important message to get across? Do you have an idea, a service or a product to sell? If you want to move ahead in your career, make the grade in class, or if you just want to give the world a piece of your mind, then you need to learn how to speak for yourself—with confidence.

This simple, straightforward guide will help you accomplish your goal and achieve a level of professionalism you never thought possible. Now you can make any audience sit up and take notice, win its admiration and applause. Bravo!

SPEAK FOR YOURSELF WITH CONFIDENCE

ELAYNE SNYDER is a respected communications consultant and educator. She has taught classes in speechmaking at New York University and The New School in New York. She has also conducted seminars around the country for numerous corporations and the United States Civil Service. Ms. Snyder lives in New York City.

SIGNET and MENTOR BOOKS for Your Reference Shelf

(0451)

- [ ] **SLANG AND EUPHEMISM by Richard A. Spears.** Abridged. From slang terminology describing various bodily functions and sexual acts to the centuries-old cant of thieves and prostitutes to the language of the modern drug culture, here are 13,500 entries and 30,000 definitions of all the words and expressions so carefully omitted from standard dictionaries and polite conversation. (118898—$4.50)*

- [ ] **THE LIVELY ART OF WRITING by Lucile Vaughan Payne.** An essential guide to one of today's most necessary skills. It illumines the uses—and misuses—of words, sentences, paragraphs, and themes, and provides expertly designed exercises to insure thorough understanding. (623851—$2.95)*

- [ ] **HOW TO WRITE, SPEAK AND THINK MORE EFFECTIVELY by Rudolf Flesch.** This renowned authority on writing offers you a complete, step-by-step course for improving your thinking, writing, and speaking abilities. A complete course in the art of communication. (141938—$4.50)*

- [ ] **THE BASIC BOOK OF SYNONYMS AND ANTONYMS by Laurence Urdang.** Expand your vocabulary while adding variety to your writing with thousands of the most commonly used words in the English language. Alphabetically arranged for quick and easy use, this indispensable guide includes sample sentences for each word. (137256—$3.50)*

*Prices slightly higher in Canada

Buy them at your local bookstore or use this convenient coupon for ordering.

NEW AMERICAN LIBRARY,
P.O. Box 999, Bergenfield, New Jersey 07621

Please send me the books I have checked above. I am enclosing $_____ (please add $1.00 to this order to cover postage and handling). Send check or money order—no cash or C.O.D.'s. Prices and numbers are subject to change without notice.

Name_____

Address_____

City_____State_____Zip Code_____

Allow 4-6 weeks for delivery.
This offer is subject to withdrawal without notice.

SPEAK FOR YOURSELF —WITH CONFIDENCE

by Elayne Snyder
with Jane Field

Illustrations by Edna Mudge McNabney

A SIGNET BOOK
NEW AMERICAN LIBRARY

NAL BOOKS ARE AVAILABLE AT QUANTITY DISCOUNTS WHEN USED TO PROMOTE PRODUCTS OR SERVICES. FOR INFORMATION PLEASE WRITE TO PREMIUM MARKETING DIVISION, NEW AMERICAN LIBRARY, 1633 BROADWAY, NEW YORK, NEW YORK 10019.

Copyright © 1983 by Elayne Snyder

All rights reserved

 SIGNET TRADEMARK REG. U.S. PAT. OFF. AND COUNTRIES
REGISTERED TRADEMARK—MARCA REGISTRADA
HECHO EN CHICAGO, U.S.A.

This book previously appeared in a Plume edition published by New American Library.

SIGNET, SIGNET CLASSIC, MENTOR, PLUME, MERIDIAN
AND NAL BOOKS are published
by New American Library,
1633 Broadway, New York, New York 10019

Library of Congress Catalog Card Number: 85-62385

First Signet Printing, February, 1986

1 2 3 4 5 6 7 8 9

PRINTED IN THE UNITED STATES OF AMERICA

To
YOU

CONTENTS

Introduction		1
Chapter 1	What You Should Know About Your Audience	5
Chapter 2	Formulating Your Speech Statement	14
Chapter 3	Patterns to Model Your Speech On	26
Chapter 4	The Snyder Four-Card Structure System	31
Chapter 5	Developing the Body of Your Speech	45
Chapter 6	Putting It All Together: A Review	57
Chapter 7	Delivery Methods and Systems	67
Chapter 8	Visual Aids	76
Chapter 9	Body Language	92

viii • Contents

Chapter 10	Rehearsal and Delivery	100
Chapter 11	Fear Is a Four-Letter Word for the Unknown	108
Chapter 12	Introducing the Speaker	117
Chapter 13	The Question and Answer Period	124
Chapter 14	"Speech! Speech!"—Impromptu Speaking	134
Chapter 15	A Speech Is a Gift—Speech Samples	143
Chapter 16	Radio and Television	159
Chapter 17	Meetings	175
Chapter 18	Formidable Formats: Workshops, Seminars, Panels	187
Chapter 19	Speakers' Smórgasbord: Answers to a Variety of Concerns	197
Chapter 20	Bravo! Brava!	205
Suggested Further Reading		207
Index		209

SPEAK FOR YOURSELF
—WITH CONFIDENCE

INTRODUCTION

MEMORANDUM   CHAPTER ONE

TO: *You*

FROM: *Elayne Snyder*

SUBJECT: *This Book—What's in it for you*

This is an unabashedly optimistic book about a fast, easy way to learn how to be an effective public speaker. It differs from other books on the subject because it shows you exactly what to do and exactly how to do it. It's loaded with useful, concrete examples to illustrate specific situations. This book offers you a system for building a memorable speech—and presenting it without having a nervous breakdown.

The first step is for you to forget everything you've heard about how frightening, mysterious, and complex public speaking is. It isn't. As a teacher and communications consultant, I am well aware of the paralyzing effect fear can have on a speaker, and have included a chapter to deal with it. But, have patience; don't immediately skip to this chapter on fear to see if my system can really work for you: I believe that the Snyder System will allay those fears before you even reach that chapter. Before then, too, you will have found out that nervousness is a positive asset—it can get your creative juices flowing, add enthusiasm to your voice, tone, and manner, and have a lively effect on your audience as well. Nervous energy is something to use, not to get rid of.

Unless you are talking to yourself, you are constantly engaged in "public" speaking. You'll be on the right, relaxed road if you think of speaking in public as just talking to more than one person. Remember that people listen one at a time, and as far as any one listener is concerned, you are speaking only to him or her as an individual. So talk to your audience that way, in an easy conversational manner, as though each person were the one-and-only and you are about to give them something they want—a gift of knowledge.

Like any gift worth giving, yours will be carefully selected, beautifully wrapped, and enthusiastically presented. It will be warmly received because you had the receiver in mind every step of the way, and the audience is numero uno in your book.

A gift is for someone you know. The better you know your audience, the more likely it is that your gift will be needed, used, and appreciated. If you don't know the receiver, you run the risk of giving chocolates to a weight watcher. That's why the audience has to be your first consideration—you *must* know to whom you are talking before you decide what to tell them.

The best gift to give is not the one you yourself would like to receive, but the one your audience wants. So put yourself in their shoes—ask yourself what you would want to hear if you were in the audience. If you are interested in solar energy and your audience is the local florists association, you can't miss if you talk about solar heat for greenhouses; whereas, your message would fall on deaf ears if you decided to talk about solar heat for igloos to these florists—no matter how fascinating it might be to you and the Aleutian Indians.

The temptation to tell everything you know about your subject has to be resisted too, not just because your time is limited, but also because the audience cannot absorb that much in one sitting. The ear is a limited learning tool—only 11 percent of what is heard is actually remembered for more than an hour. So select your target and stay on it. (The Snyder Four-Card System is designed to help you do just that. It's a quick and easy way to organize a speech on any subject for any occasion.)

If you selected the perfect gift and then stuffed it in a wrinkled old brown paper bag, it could wind up in the wastebasket by mistake. Don't run that risk with your gem of a speech. Wrap it in the definite, specific, concrete, colorful, pictorial language it deserves. Use examples, glittering images, metaphors, anecdotes, statistics, case histories, quotations. Stick to the active voice and action verbs just as you do in conversation. Colorful language is to the speaker as paint is to the artist. Use a broad palette to paint memorable pictures, something your audience will take home with them and treasure.

Once you've absorbed all of the above, have crafted a terrific speech, and have rehearsed it thoroughly, the presentation should be simply a matter of waiting for your standing ovation, right? Wrong. Murphy's Law, "Everything that can go wrong will go wrong," still applies. To combat these miserable odds you need this antidote—Snyder's Law:

> When the unexpected happens, don't agonize—improvise. Keep your cool and keep on going.

Be prepared for what might go wrong. By checking and rechecking in advance, you will not arrive on the wrong day, in the wrong place, at the wrong time. Your notes will be in order. Your slides will be right side up. Your microphone will work. There are some things that are beyond your control—but if a dog walks down the aisle, or the waiter drops a tray, or the lights go out, you'll take it in stride with Snyder's Law as your security blanket. Keep it handy.

This book will give you the tools you need, and the confidence to turn out a good speech on any subject regardless of length, time, or complexity. The Snyder System will not only serve you on the public platform, but in all areas of communications: telephone conversations, impromptu office meetings, social events, discussions with friends, your office memos, business reports, and even your personal letters. In short, the Snyder System is a blueprint for better communications of every sort. I have designed it to resemble, as much as possible, the supportive training sessions I have with adult students and the private consultations I have with individual clients. But like all real learning, public speaking proficiency comes through actual practice, and I urge you to speak at every opportunity.

1
WHAT YOU SHOULD KNOW ABOUT YOUR AUDIENCE

What you say, and how you say it, depends on your audience—whom you're speaking to. Once you receive the speech invitation, your first thought must be, "Whom will I be speaking to?" No matter what role you are invited to play—featured speaker, panelist, workshop leader, introducer/host, or any other—what you say will be determined by who is in your audience.

Knowing your audience and giving them what they want to hear is the key to effective communication on any level, whether you're talking to a small group at your office, to members of your club, or to members of the board of directors. Knowing them affects what you say and how you say it. You can't sell meat to vegetarians, snow boots to a bedouin, or wine to teetotalers. Don't even try. Instead, tell them omething you know they will find interesting, noteworthy, and thought-provoking. You will not thrill an audience of physicists with the wonders of basic math.

To find out what sort of group you will be speaking to, ask your contact person (the one who extended the speech invitation). The information she provides will enable you to size up your audience accurately and determine how to reach them, interest them, hold them, motivate them.

6 • SPEAK FOR YOURSELF WITH CONFIDENCE

Always ask your contact person specific questions. The following checklist will guide you as to general areas you should ask about. If your contact person acts surprised or impatient

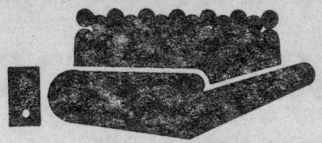

with your third-degree grill, forgive her. She will understand why later, when your audience hangs on to every word of your speech and applauds vigorously because you took the time to get to know them and prepare a speech exclusively for them.

The Know-Your-Audience Checklist

1. Find out about the *age group* you'll be speaking to. Are they young, old, middle, mixed? Age influences what your audience knows and what they're interested in. Would you speak to an audience of people in their eighties and nineties about birth control and their practice of it? Would you give a speech on retirement to teenagers? Know the age mix of your audience and save yourself from preparing the wrong speech for the wrong audience.

2. Ask your contact person about the *sex* of your audience. Will they be all men? All women? Mostly men? Mostly women?
   Women and men do not always see life's experiences from the same point of view. Knowing the sex of your audience —by asking, not assuming—will spare you surprises you can live without. Suppose you were invited to speak to an audience of coal miners and assumed they were all men. When you arrived with a speech written on the assumption they were all men, you found half were women. Don't assume. Ask.
   When you know the sex of your audience you can focus your speech to include everybody's interests, sensitivities,

expectations. You'll also know which pronoun is most appropriate to use with your audience. If your audience is all women, mostly women or some women, be sure to use "she" as well as "he" so the women and the men will know you're talking to everybody in the audience.

3. Know the *education level* of your audience. Naturally, if you're invited to speak at a college alumni association meeting, you'd already have the answer! People's comprehension is influenced by what they know. If the audience's education level is high school, you should know that—not to talk down to them, but to be sensitive to their interests and knowledge base. You can get closer to an audience's needs if you know who they are and where they're coming from. Don't patronize. Localize.

4. Know your audience's *occupation(s)*, especially if you're speaking to a professional group. Are they all government employees? All dentists? All artists? All programmers? What people do for a living colors their thinking and their listening. Find out what your audience does for a living. You might want to refer to it in your speech.

5. Know your audience's *social* and *economic background*. People from different roots and cultures have different viewpoints and expectations, and you could commit an unnecessary gaffe if you inadvertently insult your listeners. Ask in advance, and you will not offend in ignorance.

The more you know about your audience, the more likely it is that you will give them a speech that's a gift. Remember, people's interests, jobs, education, background, and community will have a significant effect on their response to you and your speech. Cater to their special interests.

As I have stressed, your best source for the information you need is your contact person. She should be able to give you all the information you'll need, or refer you to someone who can. It is important to establish a rapport with your contact early, so you will feel free to call again for any further information you need. The Know-Your-Audience Checklist will show you how to formulate a helpful audience profile, but to be completely prepared you must find out even more specific information about the conditions under which you will be speaking. Below is a list of specific questions for your contact to which you will need the answers in order to do a smooth, professional job.

FEATURED SPEAKER

If you have been invited to be the featured speaker, or one of the featured speakers, don't leave anything to chance. (For checklists for panelists and workshop seminar leaders, see Chapter 18.) Your role as a featured speaker will set the tone for all that follows. Your contact person knows that, and should outline for you all the necessary preliminaries.

Imagine that you are an executive in the world's largest business, the federal government. You work for the Small Business Administration and have been invited to address the Midwest Conference of the Association of Small Businesses in Chicago.

Before you pack your bags and head for the Windy City, before you even begin to think about your speech, you should start picking the brains of your contact person. Begin with these questions:

Featured Speakers Checklist

1. What is the purpose of the meeting/conference?
2. What topic do they have in mind for your speech?
3. Will there be other speakers? If so, who are they and what are their topics? What will be the order of speakers? Will you be speaking first?
4. How many people will attend the meeting? (If you assume it will be around two hundred people and you arrive to find two thousand, it could be unsettling.)
5. Who will be in your audience? (Answers to the Know-Your-Audience Checklist are essential.)

What You Should Know About Your Audience • 9

6. How long should your speech run? (Abide by it.)
7. Will there be a Question and Answer session? How long will it be? After each speech? After all speeches? Who will moderate it?
8. Where will you be giving your speech? An auditorium? A ballroom? A tent? (You can use this information when you're rehearsing, imagining yourself giving a wonderful presentation in that environment—it will help you handle your nervousness. The more you know, the less anxious you'll be.)
9. Is there a stage? A dais? Podium? Lectern? (Discuss what you'll need early in your conversations, and recheck in advance of your speech to be sure it will be there as you've requested.)
10. Is there a microphone? What kind: gooseneck? floor? lavaliere? (You can arrange to meet the sound person beforehand to learn about the microphone if that would make you feel more comfortable.)
11. Can you order special equipment and count on it being there? For example: overhead projector, screen, slide projector, equipment operator.
12. Confirm the date, time (and what time you should arrive), and place of the meeting. (If it is to be held at some huge complex like a college or government building, get details on the exact location and explicit, written instructions on how to get there. Request a map, especially if you're driving. All of this forethought and action will save you a lot of time and aggravation.)
13. Ask your contact person for her name (spelling), title, telephone number, and address so you can call back if you have any questions, as well as send her your biography in advance.
14. Finally, ask if there's anything else your contact feels you should know about the event or audience that would help you prepare the best possible speech for this audience.

Every audience has a different set of priorities. It's your job as speaker to know those priorities. An audience, like an

10 • SPEAK FOR YOURSELF WITH CONFIDENCE

individual, wants to be central in any communication, public or private, and only by knowing your audience can you give a successful speech. When you know them, you can select a subject you know that will touch them where they live.

Once you've done your audience research and know specifically who they will be, you are ready to move on to the creative challenge of selecting the components of your speech. The answers to the Know-Your-Audience Checklist will give you specific knowledge and insights about your audience. But before you move on to grapple with the subject of your speech, take a look at the general, the universal side of human nature by familiarizing yourself with what I call Mind-grabbers. Mind-grabbers are people-pleasers, attention-getters, fascinators. The Mind-grabbers list will open doors in your imagination, get your creative juices surging, and suggest areas of interest you can use. And, once you've decided what you're going to speak about, you can return to the Mind-grabbers list for ways to make your speech subject more meaningful to your audience, more fun to listen to. Mind-grabbers are the psychologically tested and proven things people want to hear about; once you read through the list you'll see why. Mind-grabbers are simply captivating areas of human interest (some positive, some negative, but all sure-fire) that you can use to attract and hold audience attention. Your speech will sizzle when you use them strategically, and your audience will be enthralled.

Mind-grabbers

Health—Whether you talk about good health and how to achieve it or maintain it, or bad health and how to relieve it, health is big news. Exercise, one aspect of health, is practically a sacrament these days.

Food—What's right with it. What's wrong with it. How to grow it, cook it, serve it. Some aspect is bound to be of special interest to your particular audience.

Money—How to make more of it. How to use less of it. How to invest it. How to get rich quick. Everybody is interested in money—even the rich want to get richer. As the saying goes, "One is never too rich or too thin."

What You Should Know About Your Audience • 11

Power—We all want power—even if it's limited to the "power of positive thinking." We strive to get some power over our own lives—politically, economically, socially, spiritually. We are fascinated with "the Power Elite" who control the worlds of high finance, industry, and politics. We want to know how they did it and how we can go and do likewise. We want a blueprint for $ucce$$, and any speech that offers it will have a ready audience.

People Who Have Made It—The next best thing to having money and power ourselves is hearing about those who have it. Rags-to-riches stories are irresistible. Think of the continuing interest in Elvis Presley, Marilyn Monroe, Janis Joplin, the Beatles. Or the great athletes who live out our richest fantasies: Muhammid Ali, Fernando Valenzuela, John McEnroe, Billie Jean King. And any unusual twist in the lives of such great achievers in any field is a boon for the speaker.

Sex—Almost anything about sex from "how-to" to "don't do" will get attention.

Diet—Americans are the world's fattest people, and we hate being fat. Our desire to be thin is equaled only by our passion for eating fattening food. Almost any diet gimmick suggested will be tried, so it's a sure-fire mind-grabber.

Love—Falling in or out of it. The love of children, family, friends, pets. Loving your neighbor as yourself. Libraries are filled with tomes on these subjects—and any variation on the universally popular love theme is guaranteed to win you audience interest.

Friends—*How to Win Friends and Influence People* is more than just a book title, it's a national industry. Everyone wants to get along with other people and will be interested in how to achieve it.

Stress—Any change, good or bad, is a major cause of stress. Since we all undergo changes of some sort all the time, the process has opened up a whole new field for speakers. How to deal with marriage or divorce, birth or death, being hired or fired, getting or not getting a raise are all aspects of stress, and therefore possible mind-grabbers for your speech.

Problems—People want answers to all the problems that beset them—physical, moral, ethical, religious, economic. Be sure the problem is one your audience can relate to or your speech will fall on deaf ears.

Fun—The pleasure principle applies to everybody. We all want to get more out of life. Sports, films, plays, poetry, and the visual arts are avenues to a more enjoyable life, and therefore are good mind-grabbers for successful speeches.

Adventure—Action stories fascinate people. Not just the kind that happen once in a lifetime like climbing Old Smoky or shooting the rapids in a leaky canoe, but also the larger adventure that is life: first love, first job, marriage, divorce, birth of a child. People love to hear stories about other people and their adventures.

Oddball People/Oddball Facts—The popularity of the *Guinness Book of World Records* testifies to our joy in reading about kinky things. If a man transcribes the Lord's Prayer on the head of a pin, do you ask yourself, "To what good purpose?" No, you rejoice in his feat and applaud with admiration. Anything that amazes you will amaze other people too, and therefore will make good speech material.

Dramatic Events—Especially catastrophic events command our attention—an earthquake, fire, accident, war, crime, tornado. Even old tragedies are reexamined, like the Chicago fire, the San Francisco earthquake, the sinking of the *Titanic*. Heroic deeds in the face of danger are also front-page news.

Finding out about your audience is only your starting point in the making of a speech; you must then tailor that speech to them and their interest. Your speech must answer this question in the minds of your listeners: What use is this to me? Keep that question in mind as you select what to include your speech. Ask yourself this question, too, as you

What You Should Know About Your Audience • 13

wander through your subject possibilities for your audience: If you were sitting in this audience, what would you want to know from this authority (you!)? Then, give them what they don't know and would like to know about a subject you know a great deal about.

When you finally find the perfect speech (and you will), you must let the audience know that you are addressing each of them, personally. You can do this simply by using the pronoun "you" effectively. For example: "Good evening, tonight might be the last time you drink coffee"; or "Good evening, have you ever wondered about the evolution of the stars?"; or "Good afternoon, today I'm going to tell you how to avoid getting wrinkles." Phrase your speech in immediate terms.

Now that you have a good idea of your audience, what are you going to say? In the next chapter I will explain, step by step, just how to select a single speech subject, decide on a dominant purpose, and combine your subject and purpose into a speech statement that will be the foundation for a successful speech.

FORMULATING YOUR SPEECH STATEMENT

Once you know whom you will be talking to, you have two important decisions to make—what will you talk about, and why. Subject and purpose must be intertwined if your speech is to be effective and memorable. To achieve this, combine your subject and purpose in one sentence, a speech statement, that will be the foundation for your speech. This process can be expressed by the following dynamic equation:

Subject + Purpose = Speech Statement

SELECTING A SINGLE SUBJECT

By now you should have a good idea of the general topic of the meeting or conference at which you will be speaking —assuming you have done your homework properly and established a good rapport with your contact. Narrowing down this general topic to a speech subject you can successfully focus on is harder. I cannot overestimate the importance of selecting one single subject for your speech if you

Formulating Your Speech Statement • 15

want your audience to retain what you say. So you must narrow your focus to broaden your effectiveness. A good way to start is to use the brainstorming technique—just write down everything that comes into your head on one particular subject, usually one word or a short phrase. Make no attempt to edit or refine. For example, let's say you are a nutritionist and you have been invited to speak at a community nutrition conference to an audience of two hundred well-educated men and women. None of them is an expert in the food field but all are interested citizens from the community, mostly couples in their twenties, thirties and forties. You know one thing right away: You cannot tell them everything you know about nutrition in twenty minutes. Knowing your audience will help to narrow your focus; for this group you should not cite elaborate scientific case histories as you would when talking to your peers in a health center. But you should use case histories to support a point for their human interest. So, with your audience in mind, jot down as many aspects of nutrition as you can. You should be able to come up with quite a few. Here's a sampling:

Diets: Good/Bad/Fad
Easy Menus
Vitamins
Nutrient Allowance
Deficiency Diseases
Fast Foods
Nutritious Snacks
Balanced Meals
Poor Food—Poor Health
Health Foods
Diet Analysis
High-Energy Food
Sugar/Salt/Flour
Coffee/Tea
Vegetarian

You now consider all of these topics and decide which would be the most useful to your audience. With them in mind, narrow the list. Choose two or three that you think would make the best single subjects. If they are not specific enough,

16 • SPEAK FOR YOURSELF WITH CONFIDENCE

you will have to tighten your focus to arrive at your single speech subject. High-Energy Food, Do-It-Yourself Diet Analysis, and The Truth About Vitamin C are good examples of such specific subjects. Now you're ready to make a final choice. You decide this audience would find it very useful to know how to do a diet analysis of their daily meals. Look at your choice—is it single enough? Focused enough? Once you've narrowed the focus, you're well on the way to building a successful speech.

Get in the habit of looking at any subject through the eyes of your audience. Say, for example, you are a member of the Community Rescue Squad and you have been asked to speak at the Beach and Boat Club Luncheon. You are familiar with all the functions of the Rescue Squad—ambulance service, recruiting volunteers, fund raising, and water safety—but because you know your audience are beach and boat people, you can immediately begin to narrow your focus down to "water safety." So you begin a short brainstorm and come up with:

> Life-saving Techniques
>
> Reviving the Nearly Drowned
>
> Safety Tips for Sailors
>
> First Aid for Boat People
>
> Navigation Safety Rules We Sometimes Ignore

Since any one of these would take up your allotted speech time, you must select just one. You decide to talk about reviving the nearly drowned and focus on a more specific aspect of this single subject: the use of CPR (cardio-pulmonary resuscitation) on the nearly drowned. This should be a successful speech topic because it is a new technique and probably not yet known to most of your audience.

Practice breaking down general topics into single subjects by using your own areas of expertise. Think of your audience as you write down general topics about your job and your expertise in other areas (hobbies, community involvement, and the like). Take one general area and break it down

Formulating Your Speech Statement • 17

into more focused subjects as I have done in the following examples:

Audience: PTA Members
General Topic: Local politics
Single Subject: Running for local town office
Importance of working for your party
Getting kids involved in the community
Need for community gardens
Citizens' crime patrols

Audience: High School Teenagers
General Topic: Health
Single Subject: Stop smoking!
Run for your life
Yoga for fun
Aerobic dancing
Nutrition versus junk food
Vitamins—what for?

Audience: High School Teachers
General Topic: Sexism
Single Subject: Impact of sexist language on teenagers
Effect of sexism in the workplace
Sexism in the constitution
Sexism in the Bible
Sexism in young women's self-images
Impact of sexist advertising

If you get in the habit of concentrating on specific topics in this way, you will never be at a loss for something to talk about. There are dozens of subjects for speeches in every area of your life. Narrowing your focus to suit your audience is the key. Here's how some of my clients and students focused on their single speech subjects:

Audience	General Subject Area	Single Speech Subject
College Alumni Association	→ Investing	→ Investing in municipal bonds

18 • SPEAK FOR YOURSELF WITH CONFIDENCE

Audience	General Subject Area	Single Speech Subject
Working Men and Women	Management	Negotiating for a raise
Company Middle Management Group	Accounting	Getting a bigger tax refund
Business People at YMCA Lecture Series	Stock Market	Selecting the right stock
Cat Lovers	Pet Health	Giving a cat a pill
Public Relations Club	Visual Aid Equipment	Using multimedia slide show for your clients
High School Health Education Class	Podiatry	Taking care of your feet
College Seniors	Personnel/ Recruiting	Writing a résumé

DECIDING ON YOUR DOMINANT PURPOSE

Once you have decided on your single subject, it is time to consider the *dominant purpose* of your speech. Here again, it is important to think about the purpose in terms of your audience—how do you want them to respond to what you say? You may have numerous reasons for giving your speech, but only one should be your dominant purpose, and it should be so crystal clear that you can merge it with your single subject in one short sentence.

Public speeches generally have purposes that fall into five basic categories: to inform, to convince, to impress, to move to action, and to amuse. None of these purposes is mutually exclusive. In fact, a speech might include a combination or even all five of them, but only one purpose should dominate if your speech is to bring about the response you want from your audience.

For example, let's continue with your role as speaker for the Rescue Squad to the Beach and Boat Club audience. You selected CPR for reviving the nearly drowned as your single speech subject. What response do you want from your audience? Do you want them to know all about CPR? If so, then your dominant purpose is to inform. If you want them to think the Heimlich Maneuver is superior to old methods, then your dominant purpose is to convince. After you decide on your dominant purpose, you will merge it with your single subject to form a speech statement, such as "To inform about the new Heimlich Maneuver for reviving the nearly drowned victim" or "To convince that the new Heimlich Maneuver is superior to old methods of reviving the nearly drowned." It might help to show your progression on a card:

Audience:	Beach and Boat Club
Single Subject:	The Heimlich Maneuver for reviving the nearly drowned
Dominant Purpose:	To inform
Speech Statement:	Inform about the Heimlich Maneuver for reviving the nearly drowned

And remember the speech equation:

Single Subject + Dominant Purpose = Speech Statement

You must know how to formulate a speech statement, because the speech statement is the foundation on which every speech is built. Your speech statement has been chosen with a particular audience in mind, and will determine what you say and how you say it. So keep your speech statement propped up in front of you as you gather materials for your speech; it will keep you on the track. In fact, it will actually determine what materials you need for your speech. Going back to your Beach and Boat Club speech statements, for example, you will certainly have to spend much of your time demonstrating how to do CPR if your intention is to inform, while if you want to convince, you will need data that proves CPR is superior to older methods—testimonials from doctors, lifeguards, and Rescue Squad personnel.

Obviously, there will always be some overlapping of purposes. To convince you must inform, to move to action you must convince and impress and inform, and so on. But you must have one purpose that is supreme, one that dominates your entire presentation. As I mentioned in the opening paragraph of this section, you can use two, three, four, or all five of these purposes in one speech. However if you fail to clearly emphasize one main purpose, you won't know where you are going, and neither will your audience.

It will be helpful in choosing your dominant purpose to have a good grasp of the nature of the five basic purposes of public speaking. Following is a discussion of each category and the occasions when each is most appropriate:

To inform This is the most common purpose for the majority of speeches. It is the main purpose of classroom lectures, training sessions, meetings, status reports, and public lectures on anything from solar energy and the nuclear freeze movement to filing systems and high technology. It is the main purpose of how-to speeches: how to make more money, pay lower taxes, lose more weight, gain on the stock market, and so on. Even when "to inform" is not the dominant purpose, it is always an element in any speech on any subject, since you obviously would not speak at all if you had no information to give your audience. In fact, a speech intended to convince will have to inform before it can convince. You couldn't convince an audience that CPR is superior to other methods if you didn't first inform them what it is.

Some examples of speech statements whose dominant purpose is to inform are:

Formulating Your Speech Statement • 21

How to run a good meeting.
How a law gets passed.
How to lower your blood pressure.
How to climb the corporate ladder.
How to choose the right medical plan for employees.

To convince This is the usual purpose of speakers who either want the audience to change their beliefs or to resist change being advocated by others. It is usually the dominant purpose of speeches by lawyers, politicians, salesmen, and reformers. Naturally, if you have to convince your audience of something, it implies that there is some controversy or doubt about your point of view. It is up to you as the speaker to marshal facts carefully, to back up your statements with specifics—the testimony of experts, compelling data, meaningful statistics—in order to get your audience to change their minds or to resist some change.

Here are some examples of speech statements intended to convince:

American cars are the best value.
Good nutrition is a key to cancer cure.
College football should be subsidized completely by the professional leagues.
A nuclear freeze is necessary for the survival of the planet.
Vegetarian meals can be a gourmet delight.

To impress This is the purpose of many inspirational talks to church groups, conventioneers, business associates, workers, athletes, voters, and club members. It is the standard purpose at many ceremonial events, such as graduation exercises, weddings, anniversaries, retirement dinners, and memorial services. The speech to impress reinforces shared beliefs and should contain some new information. Many speeches to impress could begin with the phrase, "Let us now praise . . ." followed by your subject: the deceased, the team, Vietnam veterans, old George who is about to retire, the scouts, the bride and groom, or your parents on their anniversary.

Following are some speech statements whose dominant purpose is to impress:

Honoring George Jones for fifty years of service to the company.
Extolling our country on the Fourth of July.
Pepping up the team to go out and win.
Congratulating the sales force for record sales.
Exhorting new graduates to reshape the world.

To move the audience to action This is the purpose of speeches that request some active participation on the part of the audience. You want them to do more than just change their opinions; you want them to actually *do* something—sign a petition, join a club, give money for a cause or a candidate. This is a very difficult undertaking that will require all your powers of persuasion. As always, know your audience. Consider your chances of success if you tried to get contributions for Planned Parenthood from an audience drawn from the Moral Majority. You might take a few hints from the advertising fraternity. Soap companies sponsor daytime soap operas because they know that's what their customers want to watch. Similarly, beer, oil, and car companies sponsor an endless variety of sports shows because they know that their customers watch those shows. By advertising on the right program, manufacturers have a captive audience for their sales pitch. As a speaker, you also have a captive audience. Just be sure your speech statement's message is the right one for your audience. A "ring around the collar" commercial beamed at football fans would not move the product off the shelf.

Here are some speech statements whose dominant purpose is to move the audience to action:

Join an antinuclear rally.
Sign a petition for your candidate.
Give blood to the blood bank.
Sign up for the Foster Grandparents Program.
Join the Neighborhood Watch crime patrol.

To amuse This is the purpose of many after-dinner speakers, toastmasters, "warm-up" speakers who precede keynote speakers, and sometimes of people who introduce other speakers. These types of speeches are by nature short, and characterized by anecdotes, jokes, humorous quotations, funny character sketches, and tall stories germane to the occasion. Such speeches are usually given by speakers well known to the audience. Television examples of this genre abound. Dean Martin's "Roasts" honor one guest who is then "roasted" by all the other guests in brief turns at the microphone. The Johnny Carson monologues are aimed at warming up the audience for his program of the evening. Since speeches to amuse are usually special-occasion speeches, make sure that your speech statement clearly indicates the occasion.

Here are a few examples:

> Anecdotes about Sally Jones's rise to power on the occasion of her becoming a senior vice-president.
> Funny mishaps in our newspaper's first one hundred years.
> Tall stories about Joe Smith's fishing prowess on the occasion of his becoming Top Worm in the Anglers' Club.
> Disasters I have shared with George and Jane Brown during the first fifty years of their marriage.

Understanding the five basic purposes of public speaking will make it much easier for you to formulate a speech statement that will address itself to a particular audience, on a particular occasion. Keep in mind the importance of selecting one of the five purposes as your dominant one, but realize that it is not your only purpose. There will always be some overlapping. For example, if your firm has just brought out the new Wonder Word Processor, your dominant purpose when you address the company sales force may be to inform them about the new product. But you may also want to convince them that it is superior to all others; move them to greater sales action in the near future; impress them with the company's achievement; and you might want to amuse them while you are doing all of the above. Just don't let the secondary purposes get in the way of your dominant purpose—in this case, to inform.

HOW TO NARROW YOUR FOCUS TO BROADEN YOUR EFFECTIVENESS

The only way to be an expert at formulating speech statements is to practice until it's second nature to you. Pretend that you have been asked to speak to a particular audience. Name the audience and write it down so you have a focus for the exercises. Start with your general topic area—the topic you have been asked to speak about. Brainstorm to come up with a number of possible single speech subjects. Select the best one for your audience. Then compose your speech statement.

Before doing the exercise to create your own speech statements, study the following examples. They illustrate how single subjects evolve into speech statements incorporating a dominant purpose. Notice, too, in the last two examples, how changing the audience changes the speech statement.

Audience	General Topic/ Subject Area	Speech Statement
College Alumni Association	Investing	Convince to invest in municipal bonds
Working Men and Women	Management	How to negotiate for a raise
Group Interested in Health	Vitamins	Convince to take vitamin C to avoid colds forever
College Seniors *versus*	Personnel/ Recruiting	How to write a winning résumé
Over Forties Club	Personnel/ Recruiting	Convince to use Outplacement Service

Public Relations Club	→ Visual Aid Equipment	→ Convince to use multimedia slide show for clients

versus

Business School Students	→ Visual Aid Equipment	→ How to use slides in a business presentation

Keep in mind while doing these exercises that the dominant purpose indicates not only how you want your audience to respond but also your own attitude toward your subject. Taking the time now to practice formulating speech statements will prepare you for all that follows. The next chapter, on patterns, will show you how your speech statement helps to determine the structure of your speech.

PATTERNS TO MODEL YOUR SPEECH ON

The appropriate pattern for your speech should grow out of your speech statement, and it will, once you are aware of what patterns are, and how useful they can be in building your speech. The most common patterns are:

> Chronological
> Topical
> Spatial (or Space Description)
> Cause/Effect
> Problem/Solution

Often, you will follow more than one of these patterns, depending on your speech statement and what it dictates, but first you should have a firm grasp of what the patterns are, and how to use them.

CHRONOLOGICAL PATTERN

This pattern puts your information in a time sequence, the natural order of dates and events: morning, noon, and night;

yesterday, today, and tomorrow; infancy, childhood, adolescence, maturity; courtship, marriage, and parenthood. Both you and your audience are accustomed to thinking in a logical time pattern, which makes this one of the easiest patterns to base your speech on.

The chronological pattern also applies to the process of doing something in sequence, so any "how to" speech could fall into this pattern: how to make cement, fudge, or wine; how to fix this and that; how to swim, play tennis, defend yourself, and so on. Anything you talk about in sequential order will fit into the chronological pattern.

Example
Speech Statement: How to inject insulin
Audience: Diabetic patients
Pattern: Chronological—You can demonstrate the process: step one, step two, step three . . .

TOPICAL PATTERN

The topical pattern is the most commonly used. It is an orderly arrangement of the main points that you will spotlight in your speech. It differs from the chronological pattern in that you decide in what order you want to present them; you could start with the most important or the least important point, depending on the dynamics you want your speech to have.

Example
Speech Statement: How to reduce tension
Audience: Small Business Owners' Association
Pattern: Topical—Give three ways to reduce tension.

SPATIAL PATTERN
(OR SPACE DESCRIPTION)

As the name implies, the spatial pattern is concerned with space, area, geography, direction. It has to do with the relation of the whole to its parts, or vice versa. The spatial pattern is highly visual. You want your audience to see what you see, so you talk about the whole picture in terms of its parts; you describe the space. One of the most common examples of the spatial pattern is one you see on television every time you watch the weather report. The weather forecaster may start with the satellite picture of the weather over the whole country; then she tells you briefly what's happening out west, down south, and how all that will affect the weather in your particular area. Sometimes she starts with the local weather, then shows you the rest of the country. Either way, you get the specifics about your own area, and you see how they relate to the country as a whole. The spatial pattern goes from the general to the particular or the other way around. It is a much-used pattern in business, too.

Example
Speech Statement: What made Brand X sales jump in June?
Audience: Management team
Pattern: Spatial—Show bar chart indicating April average sales, then bar indicating slight increase of sales in May, then on to June and what caused the spectacular rise: new advertising, new packaging, and the like.

CAUSE/EFFECT PATTERN

This is also called the causal pattern. It relates two events, one of which is the cause of the other. For instance: I fell down because the stairs were icy. Or, the road was icy—that's why I fell down. In general, any event that is reason (cause)

Patterns to Model Your Speech On • 29

for another event, or any event that is the result (effect) of another event, will fit the cause/effect pattern.

Example
Speech Statement: Why we went over budget for office supplies
Audience: Management
Pattern: Cause/Effect—We underestimated demand for new brochure; the cost of high-quality stock rose by 15 percent in the past year; we ignored policy of using both sides of paper.

PROBLEM/SOLUTION

You identify the problem and offer one or more solutions when you follow this pattern. If one of your products isn't selling as well as it did last year, you might suggest solutions, such as improving the product, running more ads, or other similar measures. This is a frequently used pattern since we all have problems that need solving, whether they are in business, in the classroom, or at home. And the pattern is ubiquitous on television: Have chapped hands? Buy Balmo. Can't make pie crust? Use Bake-It-Rite. Want to lose weight? Try fasting. In general, any time you pose a problem and offer a solution, it will fit the problem/solution pattern.

Example
Speech Statement: Managing a crisis between employees
Audience: Managers
Pattern: Problem/Solution—Cite typical problem audience might face and offer solutions.

Frequently, you may decide on one pattern and find your speech statement suggests more than one. If you can use more than one effectively, do so. Otherwise, select the pattern that most strongly develops the speech you want to give.

Example
Speech Statement: Convince audience to try scuba diving
Audience: Tour group in Florida Keys

Pattern: Chronological—The steps involved in learning scuba diving. Topical—Three great things about scuba diving. Spatial—Here's what it's like down there.

Keep in mind that all these patterns will grow out of your speech statement; it is not something you need to think about before you have worked out the speech statement. As soon as you have pinpointed what you are going to talk about, the pattern will be apparent. But you must be aware of what the possible patterns are in order to easily recognize the pattern within your speech statement, and to use that pattern as an organizational tool to build your speech in a logical way. The following exercise will develop your pattern-recognition skills. Read each speech statement, then decide which speech pattern is most appropriate to it.

Speech Statements

How to fire a subordinate

Protect your back

Guidelines for buying a house

How to improve your eyesight

Why you should join the Peace Corps

Convince to use bran

How to say no without feeling guilty

What to do if the person next to you has a heart attack

What to do about sexual harassment

How best to invest $1,000

Convince to start a success support group

Convince to answer personal classified ads

New approach to equal employment

Protect yourself against unfair landlord

Convince to volunteer as auxiliary police person

4

THE SNYDER FOUR-CARD STRUCTURE SYSTEM

Now that you have mastered the method for arriving at your speech statement (Chapter 2), and the pattern it suggests (Chapter 3), you are ready to work on the other three essential components of your speech: the introduction, the body, and the conclusion. To draw this all together for you, I have developed the Snyder Four-Card System. These four cards will be your primary tool for preparing any kind of public communication of any reasonable length for any occasion.

The four cards will be labeled:

1. Speech Statement→Audience
2. Introduction
3. Body
4. Conclusion

The material you gather during research should be listed on the appropriate card so that your are organizing the information as you go. This way, by the time you have compiled what you need, the outline of your speech will be clear. And following the system will save you a lot of time, because it will

32 • SPEAK FOR YOURSELF WITH CONFIDENCE

keep you from collecting irrelevant material, even as it reminds you of what you need.

CARD 1—SPEECH STATEMENT

```
     1
   SPEECH STATEMENT
         ↓
     YOUR AUDIENCE
```

Suppose you have been asked to give a five minute after-dinner speech to a group of consumer advocates. The dinner follows a day-long conference on the serious concerns of consumers, so your contact has asked that you be light-hearted about your subject, direct mail—not normally a very amusing topic. You decide to deal with a pet peeve about direct mail: the difficulty of getting your name off a mailing list. You merge your dominant purpose and subject in one sentence to form your speech statement: To amuse by explaining how to get your name off a mailing list without actually dying. Since that's the problem and you are going to offer solutions, you will use the problem/solution pattern. So now you have the information to fill out Card 1.

Card 1. Speech Statement
  To amuse by explaining how to get your name off a mailing list without actually dying.
  Audience: Consumer advocates
  Pattern: Problem/Solution

Keep this card in front of you as you gather information for your speech. It will be your guide for selecting all subsequent material, and will help you to eliminate whatever does not further your speech statement. The fact that a speech ought to have a beginning, a middle, and an end is at least as old as Aristotle. Despite that ancient lineage, the advice is not often followed. Years ago, in a memorandum to young reporters, Edward R. Murrow put it this way:

> First you tell them what you are going to tell them.
> Then you tell them.
> Then you tell them what you told them.

Every speech, as well as every news story, can be written according to that memorable little guide, so keep it in mind as you prepare the next three cards for your speech's introduction, body, and conclusion.

CARD 2—INTRODUCTION

```
┌─────────────────────────┐
│ 2                       │
│                         │
│      SUBJECT            │
│      PURPOSE            │
│   BACKGROUND INFO.      │
│                         │
└─────────────────────────┘
```

Tell them what you are going to tell them—and then repeat it, just in case they missed it the first time. The audience must know where you are going. Then, if necessary, give background information: who, what, when, where, why. But *only* if necessary. Your main purpose in the introduction is to get the audience's attention and introduce your subject to them. If you don't get their interest in the first thirty seconds, you'll have an uphill fight all the rest of the way. So work on

34 • SPEAK FOR YOURSELF WITH CONFIDENCE

the opening as if your whole speech depended on it—because it really does.

Although your introduction is the first thing you are going to say to your audience, it is sometimes easier to formulate a good introduction after you have completed the body of your speech. In doing your research for the body, you may come across relevant anecdotes or quotations that would be especially appropriate for an introduction. However, if you feel better knowing how you are going to start your speech, you can prepare a temporary working introduction by paraphrasing your speech statement. You can change it later if you think of a better one.

For example, here's a paraphrase of the speech statement illustrated on Card 1 in the discussion above: "How to get your name off a mailing list? If you've tried and failed, be of good cheer, there are some surefire ways to get your name off a mailing list without actually dying." Since this is a short (five-minute) speech, that's a fine introduction. It has accomplished its purpose: You have told your audience what's coming; you have repeated it to be sure they know the subject; and, you have done so in an amusing way. So write it down on Card 2:

> Card 2. Introduction
> Have you ever tried to get your name off a mailing list? If you succeeded, congratulations! You're a rare bird. If you tried and failed, be of good cheer—there are some surefire ways to get your name off a mailing list without actually dying.

There are some other ways—besides paraphrasing your speech statement—to introduce a speech. Following are some of the most commonly used introductory devices; just be sure that the one you choose relates to your speech statement.

1. Ask an Interesting Question

This is one of the best ways to begin because it immediately involves your audience. Suppose your speech statement for a job seminar speech is "to inform why applicants do not get jobs they apply for." Your introduction might be:

> "Do you know why you did not get that great job you applied for? Today, I'm going to share with you some of the possible reasons why you did not get the job."

2. Make a Startling Statement

Suppose you are addressing members of the local Safety Council, and your speech statement is "to inform them how to keep drunk drivers off the road." Your introduction might be:

> "The world is coming to an end tonight! Yes, tonight in this city, the world will end for nine victims of car accidents—and five of them will be caused by drunk drivers."

3. Appeal Directly to the Special Interest of Your Audience

Suppose you are a psychologist addressing your peers and your speech statement is "to inform them that running is one of the most effective therapies for many forms of mental illness." Your introduction might be:

> "Tonight, I'm going to tell you how to push your patients off the couch and onto the right track—a cinder track, that is. According to Acme Research Associates, running must now be considered one of the most effective therapies for many forms of mental illness. The salutary effects of running, as indicated by Acme's research with mental patients, may give you something to think about in terms of your own patients."

4. Use Visual Aids

Suppose you are a real estate agent addressing a group of young marrieds, and your speech statement is "to convince them that they should buy a house now." Your introduction might be:

> Begin by taking a dollar bill out of your wallet. Hold it up for all to see, then tear it in two, and say, "This is what you are doing if you pay rent for an apartment or a house. Even at today's high interest rates, you should consider buying your own home."

A word of caution about visual aids—be sure they are visible to everyone in your audience. Otherwise, they're not an aid, they're a handicap.

5. Tell a Story, Anecdote, or Personal Experience

These are all good ways to begin, as long as they are relevant to your speech statement. Don't tell a joke or anecdote just to get a laugh; it must suit both the mood and subject of your speech statement or it will distract your audience's attention from your subject. Here's an example from one of my students whose speech statement was "to inform my peers about the art of lying." Here's her introduction:

> "I was introduced to you as Madeline Bennett, but my full name is actually Madeline Astor Bennett. The reason I leave out the Astor connection is because people immediately start asking about my robber baron ancestors, and they also begin to see dollar signs and family crests instead of me. Can you think of some other reason why I might leave it out? It's not modesty or humility. No, the reason I don't claim the Astor name is because it is not my name. I was lying to you, and the art of lying is what I will talk about today."

6. Do Something to Arouse Curiosity

Arousing curiosity is easy. The trick is to relate it to your speech statement. If you don't do that, it's a comedian's gimmick—like a false nose or a funny hat. So be sure that whatever you do to arouse curiosity is directly concerned with your speech statement. For example, suppose you have been asked to speak to a group of personnel directors who do the hiring or promoting in large corporations. Your speech statement is "to inform how to overcome visual and emotional reactions to the handicapped to insure fair employment practices." Your introduction could start with this silent action:

> You enter on crutches. You slowly, and apparently painfully, make your way to a chair that is upstage from the lectern—about twelve paces away. (You have previously put your notes on the chair.) When you get to the chair, you carefully prop the crutches up against the chair, pick up your notes, and walk briskly to the lectern. You look around at your surprised audience and then begin, "I had two reasons for pulling that stunt. First, to show you that a highly visible handicap commands your attention. But what you see is the handicap, not the person. The second reason is more subtle. When you saw that I was not handicapped, you reacted with relief. You no longer had to feel pity.
>
> "These two factors, high visibility and pity, are among the leading causes of discrimination against the handicapped person, because both happen before qualifications for a job can be considered. My talk today will be on ways to overcome both the visual and emotional first impressions in hiring handicapped employees."

7. Quotations

Look for fresh ones. Those from *Bartlett's* are often too familiar, and more often too outdated for our times. Get in the habit of writing down insightful things your friends say or statements that strike you as quotable from newspapers, magazines, periodicals, and books. Jot down memorable lines said by radio or TV personalities or their guests. Use your local library to consult some of the newer books of quotations (*The Quotable Woman* or William Safire's *Good Advice* are good ones). Whatever your source, be sure the quote is relevant to your speech statement. For example, suppose you're addressing men and women about to graduate from college and your speech statement is "how to handle a job interview." Your introduction might be:

> "The novelist John Steinbeck said, 'There are only four approaches to knowing a man: What does he look like? What has he done? What does he say—in other words think—and last, and most important, what has he done to or for me?' By adapting these four approaches to the specifics of each of your job interviews you can be sure of making the kind of first impression you want to make—a good one. So today we'll paraphrase Steinbeck and discuss:
> What should you look like?
> What have you done?
> What should you say to reveal what you think?
> What can you do for the company?"

Whichever of these devices you choose as your opening gambit, remember that your introduction must accomplish two things: (1) it must relate to your speech statement, and (2) it must tell your audience what to expect in the rest of your speech.

CARD 3—BODY

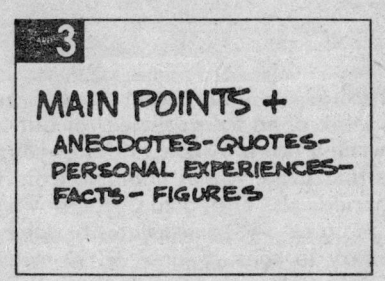

```
3
MAIN POINTS +
 ANECDOTES-QUOTES-
 PERSONAL EXPERIENCES-
 FACTS - FIGURES
```

Now is your chance to tell them what you promised to tell them. The body of your speech must be aimed at your particular audience and must fulfill the requirements of your subject and purpose as indicated in your speech statement. And, of course, the body must fulfill the promise of your introduction.

In the body of your speech, the big challenge is to organize your material into two, three, or at the most, four main points. Each point should explain, expand, or enhance the goal described by your speech statement. Each point should tell your audience what they need, want, and expect to hear about your subject. And because you want your audience to remember your main points, you must not distract them with too much information. Be selective. Decide on your main points and write then down in complete sentences. (Together they will serve as your outline, discussed further in Chapter 7). But let's continue to work with the example we used to develop cards 1 and 2, to see how best to choose and arrange these main points. The speech is to be an informative, light-hearted, after-dinner talk, and your speech statement dictates that you give your audience useful information about how to get their names off a mailing list. Since your whole speech will be only 5 minutes long, you will probably have time to cover just two main points. You have decided to use the problem/solution pattern so that each point will resolve some part of the problem. Remember, each point should be expressed in a complete sentence.

Card 3. Body
1. How to make it too expensive to keep you on their list by returning merchandise at their expense, using their prepaid envelopes to request removal, changing your address to a hamlet in Tibet.
2. How to code all future direct mail purchases and donations so you will know who is selling your name to whom.

In the next chapter, we will go into the development of material following these main points. For point 1, you need some data about the costs of mailing lists, postal regulations for returning merchandise, cost to companies of using the prepaid envelopes, and cost of changing your address. For point 2, you will have to explain how to code your mail order purchase in order to find out who is selling the list that contains your name.

The number and order of your points in the body of your speech will change according to the length of your speech and the pattern you have selected for your speech statement. In the following examples, you have twenty minutes in which to speak, so you have time for three or four main points.

Speech Statement: How to become a wine expert.
Audience: Men and women at a wine tasting party for aspiring aficionados.

"How to" indicates that an informative speech will follow. The topical pattern is obvious in the speech statement, so you arrange your points as follows:

1. Table Wines: what they are.
2. Bubblies: what they are.
3. Flavored wines: what they are.

If you were to change your speech statement to "When to serve which wines," the most logical pattern would be chronological, and your main body points would be:

1. Wines to serve before dinner.
2. Wines to serve during dinner.
3. Wines to serve after dinner.

By changing the speech statement to "Regional differences in American wines," you change to the spatial pattern. Your main body points would reflect the regions:

1. Eastern wines of the Hudson Valley and the Finger Lakes.
2. Midwestern wines of the Ohio Valley.
3. California wines—northern and southern districts.

If you change your speech statement to inform your audience why the vintage of French wines is so important, while the vintage of California wines hardly matters, your speech pattern will change, to that of cause and effect. The main points for this speech statement would be:

1. Weather determines the quality of a vintage.
2. French weather is variable so vintage is crucial.
3. California weather is comparatively constant, so vintage is not a big factor.

As the above examples indicate, once you change your speech statement you have to rethink the pattern for your speech, since the pattern will help you select suitable points of information. Discovering the appropriate speech pattern helps you collect the material you need to back up each point, because the pattern actually tells you what kind of data you need.

You now have a structure for the body of your speech, and can begin to gather relevant material without wasting time on material that doesn't fit your main points. You will expand and develop each point so that it, like the whole of your speech, will have a beginning, a middle, and an end. The techniques for developing the points in the body of your speech are numerous. Depending on your audience and your speech statement, you can use a variety of verbal and visual specifics such as statistics, case histories, comparisons, examples, visual aids, demonstrations, or combinations of these. The details of these methods will be covered in the next chapter, which is devoted to developing the body of your speech.

CARD 4—CONCLUSION

```
4
ZAP!
REMEMBER
KNOW
DO
```

Now you recap what you've told them—and that's all. Do not introduce new material or decide to make one more point. This is the time to wrap up your speech so your audience will remember what you want them to remember. It's your last chance to nail down your message in a memorable way—and it should be done with dispatch.

As with the introduction, the conclusion of your speech can also be a paraphrase of your speech statement. Or your conclusion can be a comment on what you have already told them, as in this conclusion for the speech on how to get your name off a mailing list:

Card 4. Conclusion
After trying all these ploys, you may just decide that dying is easier. But if dying seems a bit extreme, you might consider getting a larger mailbox or a larger wastebasket—or both.

Some of the other devices suggested for the introduction can be adapted for the conclusion, too, especially quotations, anecdotes, and appeals for action. But the most useful and the easiest way to wrap up your speech is exclusively a conclusion technique: the summary of your main points. You just restate them, 1-2-3, and sign off. For example, here's a possible summary for the speech on vintage wines:

"Remember, if you haven't had time to bone up on French vintage years, there are three good reasons why you should opt for California wine instead: 1. Weather affects the quality of grapes and therefore of wine; 2. French weather is variable so you must know which were vintage years; 3. California weather is consistently good for grapes, and, therefore, the California wines do not vary from year to year as much as the French."

I would like to caution you here once again about the use of anecdotes in speeches. If you use an anecdote, be sure it's relevant to your speech as a whole. Using just any story to get yourself off the stage can be very confusing to your audience, even if the story in itself is amusing. A student of mine once gave a speech on how to evaluate a résumé. Everything went smoothly until she got to the conclusion. Then, instead of ending her talk with something germane, she told an absolutely irrelevant story about wood nymphs in Wales! Never do that. Never. Be relevant, be brief, and be gone.

For a quick review of the Snyder Four-Card System, here are the assembled cards for our illustrated examples of the five-minute after-dinner speech. Note that you now have a good outline for your speech:

CARD 1. SPEECH STATEMENT
   To amuse them by explaining how to get their names off a mailing list without actually dying.
   Audience: Consumer advocates

CARD 2. INTRODUCTION
   Have you ever tried to get your name off a mailing list? If you succeeded, congratulations! You're a rare bird. If you tried and failed, be of good cheer—there are some surefire ways to get your name off a mailing list without actually dying.

CARD 3. BODY
   1. Make it too expensive to keep you on their mailing list at their expense: Use their prepaid envelopes to request removal; change to remote address in Tibet.
   2. Code all future direct mail purchases, donations, and subscriptions so you know who is selling your name to whom.

CARD 4. CONCLUSION
   After trying all these ploys, you may just decide that dying is easier. But if you're not quite ready for that, just consider getting a larger mailbox or a larger wastebasket—or both.

In the above example, the introduction is a paraphrase of the speech statement. If in developing material for your body points, your research turns up some especially apt quotations or anecdotes, you can always change it. But starting with a paraphrase of the speech statement leaves you free to get on with the central part of your speech—that is, developing your main points. Keep in mind that your main points are right next to your speech statement in importance. The body, therefore, must get most of your preparation time, which is why the next chapter will be devoted to developing the main points in the body of your speech.

5

DEVELOPING THE BODY OF YOUR SPEECH

The method for selecting the main points of the body of your speech was covered in Chapter 4. How well you develop these main points will determine whether or not your audience will understand and appreciate what you have to say. You have the skeleton of your speech; now it's a matter of putting flesh on those bare bones.

It is important to back up your three or four main points with in-depth information. Build on each point with concrete material from your own knowledge and experience; by doing research in libraries; reading newspapers, magazines, or periodicals; taking notes on relevant radio and television programs; interviewing experts in the field of your subject; and using any other good source you can tap.

Each point is like a mini-speech, with an introduction, a body, and a conclusion of its own. And, of course, each point must flow smoothly into the next so your audience can follow you. Listeners anticipate your reasoning and logic, and you must not disappoint them with insufficient or inappropriate information.

The more specific and concrete you can be in backing up your main points, the better your chances of delivering your message in an interesting and memorable way. There are several different kinds of information you can use in developing the body of a speech, and being aware of these sorts of materials will help you direct your research in an efficient way. The following is a list of such developmental materials —your speech specifics.

SPEECH SPECIFICS

Anecdotes and Narratives

An anecdote is a brief narrative that clarifies or emphasizes some point you want to make. Anecdotes are often humorous, and always short. Narratives serve the same purpose, but are more detailed, and therefore reserved for longer speeches. Any story you tell to illustrate a point, whether it is a personal experience, someone else's experience, or something you make up to suit the material, is an anecdote or a narrative. If you were talking, for instance, about the importance of knowing the Heimlich Maneuver to prevent choking, you might relate a personal experience in which you actually saved a life by performing the maneuver on a choking dinner companion.

Personal Experience

Your own knowledge of a subject is good backup for any material. For example, if you are giving a speech on how a law gets passed, and you have been personally involved in the process as a lobbyist or as a concerned citizen, you can use your own experience to describe the step-by-step process. Personal experience establishes credibility and authority with your audience.

Examples

There is no better way to get attention than to say, "For example . . ." This tells people something concrete is coming,

Developing the Body of Your Speech • 47

and they will want to hear it. This book is full of "for examples," because this is the accepted phrase with which to begin a word picture that illustrates your point. Hypothetical or fictional examples can work just as well as real examples, and often serve your purpose better because you invent and tailor the example to suit your needs. If you were talking to members of the Energy Commission, and you wanted them to think about the polluting effects of oil, you might paint them this picture:

> "Assume for the moment that enormous amounts of oil start gushing up out of the Grand Canyon and threaten to reduce the mighty Colorado River to black sludge. Would you be so delighted about the discovery of this new and potentially rich oil field that you would ignore the submersion of the canyon itself, and the devastation the pollution of the river would cause in the Southwest? Would a canyon full of crude be worth it?"

Comparisons

Comparisons are very effective because people learn more quickly when something unknown is compared with something familiar. For example, do you know what a Jerusalem artichoke is? It looks like ginger root or a gnarled white potato, and tastes like a cross between a turnip and a potato. Now you know what a Jerusalem artichoke is!

Statistics

Statistics are an effective way to back up facts, but be careful to give only figures that can be readily remembered, unless you use a visual aid or supply a handout later on. For example, suppose Franklin Roosevelt had said, "There are 51,576,298 people who are ill fed; 49,327,846 who are ill housed; and 50,221,989 who are ill clothed." Would anyone have remembered? What he did say was, "One-third of the nation are ill fed, ill clothed, and ill housed," which is easy to remember and very effective.

Case Histories

Case histories are made up of information one gathers about an individual, a company, or a product. If you are giving a speech about new products, you might use this example: Procter & Gamble didn't know they had invented a floating soap with Ivory until their customers told them. They looked into it and discovered their soapmaker had let too much air into the formula; that's how Ivory Soap was born.

Visual Aids and Demonstrations

These are effective only when they are both visible and relevant to your speech. They work best when they are necessary to make your point. If you were giving a speech about why the ostrich has become an endangered species, it would be useful and important to show the enormous size of the ostrich egg, because its high visibility makes the egg vulnerable to preying birds and animals. If you were a dancer and the subject of your presentation was a new dance step, a demonstration of that new step would be the most concrete and memorable way of doing it.

Definitions

Anything that might be unknown or misunderstood by your audience should be defined. If, for example, you were speaking to a group of people who do not use computers or do not know much about them, you would have to define some of your terms. If you were talking about computer language and used the jargon "COBOL," you would be wise to define it: COBOL is an acronym for Common Business Oriented Language.

Quotations and Opinions

Quotations and opinions from experts in the field of your subject lend authority to your statements and are, therefore, invaluable. Be sure to quote accurately and give credit to the source. For example, if you were giving a speech about the absence of women authors in literary annals, you might use this famous quote from Virginia Woolf as one explanation for that absence:

"I would venture to guess that Anon, who wrote so many poems without signing them, was often a woman."

Description

Describe a person, place, or object to get your listeners close to it. Put them in the picture. If, for example, you were in the travel business and said to a client, "St. Thomas is beautiful; you should go there," you would get little response. But if you said, "I was in St. Thomas about this time last year, and I stayed in a charming old guest house that hung over the side of the mountain and looked out over the bay below. In the evenings white cruise ships docked outside my window. The lights on their masts twinkled like a necklace of fireflies," that might get them to buy a ticket.

Handouts

Never give them out before or during your speech, because the audience will read them instead of listening to what you are saying. However, if you are giving a speech that requires statistics or charts, promise the audience that you will give them the data after your talk so they will not have to spend their time taking notes. There may be times when the nature of your speech suggests that you distribute the handout before your speech. Don't. It's far better in such cases to use your handout as a visual aid during your speech —project it before your audience on a slide or overhead projector. Refer to it. They'll get their copies later. If your handout is a questionnaire or something that requires filling out and returning, then hand it out at the appropriate moment and collect it before you move on in your presentation.

Repetition and Restatement

Remember that oral communication is the least effective learning tool. People only remember about 11 percent of what you say an hour after they hear it. Therefore, it is necessary to repeat and/or rephrase the main points of your speech. Help your audience remember.

Transitions

Smooth transitional phrases or sentences should set off the different parts of your speech as well as the main points. Transitions are signposts that tell your audience where they have been and where they are going:

I've shown you how, now I'm going to show you why. . . .
In addition to what I've already covered, this is also a consideration. . . .
Since we've already covered such and such, let's look at this and that. . . .
Now that you've seen that, you'll see how this relates. . . .

Figures of Speech

Figures of speech are special methods for improving the style of your speech. The following are some of the most common and useful ways to add color and memorability to your speech:

SIMILES are comparisons between two things that are not usually compared. The resemblance is usually stated by using the words "like" or "as."
Examples: "A speech is like a voyage."
"He's as rich as Rockefeller."

METAPHORS differ from similes in that a metaphor does not use the words "like" or "as." It states that one thing *is* another.
Examples: "A speech is a voyage."
"He's a tiger."

Mixed metaphors are a problem. If you say, "He's a tiger on the pitcher's mound with windmilling arms firing bullets like a bat out of Hades," it would be hard to grasp your meaning. However, two different metaphors in one sentence can be effective and accentuate your meaning, as in "He's a tiger at work but a cocker spaniel at home."

Alliteration

Alliteration is the repetition of sounds at the beginnings of words or in accented syllables. It is a favorite device of poets and of advertising copywriters because it is an aid to memory, and should be considered by speakers for the same reason. Avoid tongue twisters, of course, like "Peter Piper picked a peck of pickled peppers."

Examples: "Wonder Woman"
"The Masculine Mystique"

Allusion

An allusion is a reference to something you know your audience knows.

Examples: "The days of wine and roses are over."
"She's a new Edith Piaf."
"He fired employees like Attila the Hun."

Personification

Personification endows inanimate objects, abstractions, and animals with human characteristics and feelings.

Examples: "Money speaks."
"The ocean roared."
"The trees trembled."

Common or not, personification is sometimes helpful to the speaker as a way of quickly delineating characteristics that are well known and applying them to relatively unknown animals or objects.

Onomatopoeia

Onomatopoeia suggests the sense of a word by its sound: buzz, burble, bang, boo, hiss, sizzle, frazzle, razzle-dazzle, chirp, coo, moo, drone, groan, moan, and so on. Such words add color and feeling to language, and extend your meaning beyond the word itself. "He droned on and on" says a lot more than "He talked on and on." The word "drone" implies monotony, boredom, and tedious mediocrity. "She cooed with pleasure" adds a dimension that's missing in "She responded with pleasure."

Hyperbole

Hyperbole has been described as lying without deceiving. When you say, "I was in heaven," or "They've got money to burn," you don't expect anyone to take you literally. In advertising, the practice is known as "allowable puffery"; no one expects you to say your product is second-rate. The same might be said for those who support political candidates, points of view, and anything else.

Developing the Body of Your Speech • 53

Antithesis

Antithesis is juxtaposing contrasting ideas in a parallel arrangement of words or phrases. It is among the most common and most useful devices for speakers. President Kennedy used it to great effect in his memorable statements: "Ask not what your country can do for you, but what you can do for your country," and "Let us never negotiate out of fear, but let us never fear to negotiate."

Parallelism

Parallelism requires a similarity of structure in words, phrases, clauses, or sentences. Parallel structure is helpful to the speaker because it alerts the audience to what is coming next and, therefore, makes the points more obvious. It also gives your prose a rhythm that adds emotional impact to what you say. "Thy kingdom come/Thy will be done," and "The power and the glory" are good examples from the Lord's Prayer. And from the Gettysburg Address: "We cannot dedicate; we cannot consecrate; we cannot hallow this ground . . ." Note that the previously mentioned antithesis is a form of parallelism.

Oxymorons

These are seemingly contradictory words that have the effect of a paradox. Some examples are: "In deafening silence," "cruel kindness," "a cheerful pessimist," "a glorious failure," and "harmonious discord."

Rhetorical Questions

These are not really questions since the answer is implied in the question. Rhetorical questions are phrased in extremes for emphasis. Some examples include: "Shall we all go to the moon to escape pollution?" "Do we want a red flag over the White House?" "Would any sensible person opt for Armageddon?"

Because there are so many decisions to be made in selecting and using materials for your speeches, starting a speech file is almost a necessity. According to Ted Sorensen, who was John F. Kennedy's speech writer, Kennedy himself kept voluminous files. He collected stories and anecdotes, and was a prodigious clipper of articles from newspapers and magazines. All you need to begin is a manila envelope or file folder in which to stash clippings and notes that are relevant to your likely topics for speeches. The work will pay off in giving you ready access to facts you might otherwise have to research.

Use speech specifics I have just detailed to build up your entire speech from beginning to end. An appropriate quote or anecdote can give your introduction just the right impact, and a well-chosen speech specific can help you conclude memorably. Most of all, speech specifics will help you flesh out the body of your speech so that the main points you make will be retained by your audience. Speech specifics are like putting color slides in the minds of your listeners. Below is a complete speech outline used by one of my students that incorporates many of our speech specifics.

CARD 1
 Speech Statement: To inform about the mysteries of computer language
 Audience: Non-computer business people
 Pattern: Topical

CARD 2
 Introduction: The speaker tells the audience that he is going to talk about computer language and that he has ten years' experience in the computer field.

CARD 3
 Body:
  Main Point 1—Programming language called "BASIC" is used in many different applications that include accounts receivable and personnel.
   Speech Specifics

Developing the Body of Your Speech • 55

   a. Visual Aid—Show BASIC acronym
   b. Definition—Beginners All Symbolic Instruction Code
   c. Case History—How Company X used it
 Main Point 2—Programming language called "FORTRAN" is used in scientific community.
   Speech Specifics
   a. Visual Aid—Show FORTRAN acronym
   b. Definition—Formula Translation
   c. Anecdote
 Main Point 3—Programming language called "COBOL" is used by businesses for banking applications and payroll systems.
   Speech Specifics
   a. Visual Aid—Show COBOL acronym
   b. Definition—Common Business Oriented Language

CARD 4
 Conclusion: Personal experience in computer language.

In the example just outlined, the speaker used similar specifics to flesh out all three points (visual aid and definition). The approach worked very well, because it helped his audience see, remember, and understand what he was talking about. Here's another brief outlined example to illustrate the use of some of the other speech specifics:

CARD 1
 Speech Statement: How to eat with chopsticks
 Audience: Tour group on their way to Peking
 Pattern: Chronological

CARD 2
 Introduction: The speaker tells the audience to prepare themselves to eat with chopsticks on the tour, and refers to his Chinese heritage.

CARD 3
 Body:
  Main Point 1—Why the Chinese use chopsticks.
   Speech Specifics
    a. Demonstration—How to handle and manipulate them

56 • SPEAK FOR YOURSELF WITH CONFIDENCE

       b. Anecdote—Table manners in China
   Main Point 2—Foods you will have to eat with chopsticks.
     Speech Specifics
       a. Description—Cuts, colors, and textures
       b. Visual Aid—Accompanying the description

CARD 4
Conclusion
Review of demonstration and good wishes for successful trip in English and Chinese.

You now know exactly how to proceed with your speech, and can begin to write it all out with confidence. The next chapter will be a quick review of all the procedures up to this point. It will be a good checklist for your future great speeches!

PUTTING IT ALL TOGETHER: A Review

6

Now that you know the key ingredients of a speech, you're ready to put them all together to create a first-rate presentation focused on the needs and expectations of your audience. Let's run through everything together to be sure you own the method.

For this quick review, imagine that you have been invited to speak at a job seminar and have already established a good rapport with your contact person. The following discussion outlines how you should proceed.

STEP ONE—YOUR AUDIENCE
(Refer to Chapter 1)

Your audience is your first concern. Who are they? Ask about age, sex, occupation, education, special interests. Why are they attending this particular meeting? What's in it for them?

STEP TWO—GENERAL SUBJECT AREA
(Refer to Chapter 2)

What should you talk about to this audience? You need a subject that will appeal to their interests—in this case, their jobs or lack of them. Because you know their main interest is themselves, that's where your speech should be aimed. Everything you say should be audience-oriented. Liberally use the words "you" and "your" to keep you close to their interest areas.

STEP THREE—SPECIFIC SPEECH SUBJECT
(Refer to Chapter 2)

You have already narrowed your subject area because you know where your audience interest lies. They are all job seekers. You know that to get their attention you will have to talk about jobs—how to get jobs if they are unemployed or how to get better ones than they have now. But employment per se is too big a topic. You can't cover it all in five minutes, so you must narrow your focus and zero in on one aspect of job hunting. So you brainstorm. You consider talking about these possible single speech subjects: 1) handling the interviewer's questions; 2) preparing questions about the company to ask the interviewer; 3) mistakes most interviewees make; 4) turning interview negatives into positives; 5) preparing to sell yourself in the interview using the PAR method.

You decide to talk about the last one: preparing for a job interview using the PAR method. PAR is an acronym for Problem-Action-Result. It's a neat and effective method for the interviewee to use in selling herself to the interviewer. So the business problems, actions, and results you think this audience would find useful will form a significant part of your speech.

STEP FOUR—DOMINANT PURPOSE
(Refer to Chapter 2)

Do you want to inform, to convince, to impress, to move to action, or to amuse? It is obvious from your subject that in this instance you mainly want to *inform* this audience about using the PAR method in a job interview.

STEP FIVE—SPEECH STATEMENT
(Refer to Chapters 2 and 4)

You now merge subject and purpose into one sentence to get your speech statement, which will be your guide for your whole speech: How to use the PAR method in a job interview. With the completion of your speech statement you will have the information you need to fill in the first of the four cards in the Snyder Four-Card System.

Card 1. Speech Statement
   How to use the PAR method in a job interview.
   Audience: Job seekers/adults of both sexes

Remember to keep this card propped up in front of you during all subsequent preparations. It will remind you that all the material you collect for your speech must relate to your speech statement, and to your audience.

STEP SIX—INTRODUCTION
(Refer to Chapter 4)

The introduction to your speech must tell your audience what you are going to talk about. It must be attention-getting, audience-centered, interest-packed, mind-grabbing, and, of course, it must relate to your speech statement. If starting a speech is difficult for you, don't fret. You can devise a temporary introduction by paraphrasing your speech statement. Make a note of this on Card 2, like this:

Card 2. Introduction
   Paraphrase speech statement.

In the PAR speech, for example, you might say, "Tonight I'm going to tell you about an effective way to sell yourself in a job interview. The method is called PAR, P-A-R, which is short for Problem, Action, Result. A PAR is a little story of accomplishment that you use to promote yourself. Here's how it can work for you. . . ."

This paraphrase is a perfectly good opening, but you might decide you need something a little more dramatic. You could start with a visual aid, perhaps a flip chart with a big P A R printed on it, and involve your audience by pointing to the chart as you begin your speech, "This is a magic little word—P-A-R, PAR. Golfers among you will associate PAR with golf scores, but tonight I'm going to teach you a new meaning of this little word. From now on, PAR will be short for Problem-Action-Result [Flip chart to show those words] . . . a new method to help you sell yourself in a job interview."

You can also, of course, leave your introduction until after you have completed work on the body of your speech. Just because it will be the first thing you say to your audience doesn't mean that it is necessarily the first thing you must prepare. A temporary introduction may be helpful in that it will set up the transition for the main part of your speech, the body.

STEP SEVEN—BODY
(Refer to Chapters 3, 4, and 5)

The body of your speech is the largest part and will take most of your time and attention. Your first job is to decide which pattern is best suited to your speech statement. Should it be chronological, topical, spatial, cause/effect, or problem/solution? Examine your speech statement and decide. In the PAR example, the topical pattern—that is, an orderly arrangement of points—seems best. You are now ready to decide on your main points. Do your brainstorming first and list everything of importance to your subject, but select no more than three or four main points. In the PAR example, selecting the points is fairly easy: 1) how PAR works; 2) how to write a PAR; and 3) how to use PAR in job interviews. Write these points down on Card 3.

Card 3. Body
   Points 1. How PAR works
         2. How to write a PAR
         3. How to use PAR in job interviews

Keep this card in front of you as you consider what speech specifics you could use to flesh out the body. Go through the list of possibilities suggested in Chapter 5. Keep in mind that each point is a mini-speech in itself. In the PAR speech, for example, you might use these speech specifics to back up your three main points:

1. Visual aid
   Definition
2. Visual aid
   Examples
   Demonstrations

3. Rhetorical question
   Example
   Visual aid

Jot these specifics down on your body card so you will remember what you are looking for as you begin your research. You will, of course, begin with your own knowledge of the subject, and then use outside resources, including the library, the media, and interviews with people who have had similar experiences or with experts in the field. This should be your standard procedure in researching all your speeches.

In the PAR speech, you can rely almost entirely on your own experience to flesh out your points. Let's say that you use the second introduction suggested above, which ends with your displaying the flip chart with the PAR definition spelled out. You might go on to begin the body like this:

Body Point 1

You inform your audience, "Sometimes when you go for an interview, you are so keyed up that you may forget one vital fact—the person who interviews you is interested in what you can do for the company, not what the company can do for you. To help you remember that, here's a paraphrase of a famous line: Ask not what the company can do for you, but what you can do for the company. PAR will help you explain what you have already done for other companies in similar situations.

"Here's how it works [show the same visual aid you used in your opening, with the acronym PAR and the words Problem-Action-Results]: Problem . . . Action . . . Results. These three little words are par for the course (pardon the pun) in everybody's life. In every situation you are confronted with problems to solve—in your personal life as well as in your business life.

"The fact is, if you can identify a problem that you have encountered, describe the action you took to solve that problem, and explain the result, you will be able to demonstrate your concrete accomplishments to an interviewer."

You have now completed Point 1; you have told how PAR works. You started with a little introduction to motivate your audience by explaining the psychological need for PAR. You explained PAR with a visual aid, and you defined the terms so all would understand. You are now ready for Body Point 2.

Body Point 2

In this part of your speech, too, you could use visual aids such as a blackboard, flip chart, or newsprint pad displayed so all can see, with PAR written across the top and the words Problem, Action, and Result underneath. You could then proceed by saying, "Here's all you need to write your own PARs—a sheet of paper divided into three columns headed Problem, Action, Result. First, you list the problem. Then describe the action you took. And finally, write down the results of your action.

"By way of example, let's say you work in the fiscal department of your company. You noticed that absenteeism has increased at an alarming rate. [Write this down under Problem.] You suggested that employees with perfect attendance each month be rewarded with a cash bonus of half a day's pay. [Write down "Bonus for perfect attendance" under Action.] After six months, absenteeism dropped by 17 percent. [Write down "Absenteeism declined 17 percent" under Result.] And that's your PAR, an easy-to-remember achievement that demonstrates your ingenuity in resolving a problem to a prospective employer."

You can go on: "Here's another one. You noticed that printing bills for stationery and forms were going up, although you were still using the same printer and your orders had not increased. [Write down "rising printing bills" under Problem.] You decided to ask for bids from other printers on your next order. [Write that down under Action.] You discovered when the bids were in that your regular printer was 78 percent higher than the low bid, and you saved the company $2800 on the order. [Write that down under Results.] So, there's another PAR that will impress an interviewer with your ability to save money for the company by your initiative and creative thinking.

"As you can see, the trick in writing your PARs is to be specific. You focus on one problem, the action you took, and the results. You write down a separate PAR for every sticky problem that you resolved. You can easily review this list before going for an interview so that everything will be fresh in your mind, ready to be used to convince your interviewer that you are the person for the job."

You have now completed Point 2 of the body; you have shown the audience how to write PARs, and have used a visual aid to demonstrate your clear examples. On to Point 3 of the body.

Body Point 3

You might now continue: "How will knowing your PARs help you impress your interviewer? By being able to give clear responses to queries about your ability to perform, even when they are asked in such oblique ways as, 'What do you consider your strengths?' Instead of answering with a generality, you can instantly cite a PAR that will prove your skill [use same visual aid as in introduction]. Here's yet another example:

P—"One of our clients wanted a quick phone survey on the effectiveness of an ad we had placed for them. But we had a problem—not enough staff for the job.

A—"I decided to ask the local college's advertising class for help. The professor of the advertising course was delighted at the opportunity for his students to get practical business experience.

R—"Five very bright students completed the poll in two days, and we had a very satisfied client."

That completes the body of your speech. You opened with a rhetorical question: How will knowing your PARs help you impress your interviewer? You answered the question with an example using the visual aid to display your PAR.

STEP EIGHT—CONCLUSION
(Refer To Chapter 4)

Now all you need is the conclusion. Remember, this is your last chance to drive home your message, and you must be brief and to the point. Your conclusion must not contain any new facts—just tell them what you told them. Again. One of the easiest and best ways to do this is to summarize your main points. Make a note on Card 4 like this:

Card 4. Conclusion
   Summarize.

In the PAR speech, you might say: "The beauty of the PAR method is its simplicity. With what you know right now, you can create PARs that will be invaluable in your next job interview. All you need to do is remember these three steps [use the visual aid from your introduction]:

"Isolate the problem you have solved;

"describe the action you took;

"and explain the result of your action.

"With your PARs at the tip of your mind, you will never be at a loss for words. It's a surefire method for putting yourself across in any job interview. Guaranteed!"

STEP NINE—PRESENTATION

Note that the PAR speech is now a complete manuscript for a five-minute speech. This does not mean that every speaker must write out every word of a speech. Some do, but many more find it inhibits them when they get up to speak, because they are trying to remember exactly what they wrote instead of concentrating on their presentation. If you do write your speech out completely, *do not read it* to your audience. The next chapter will deal with various methods for helping you deliver your speech effectively, using notes, outlines, pictographs, and other aids.

This quick review of how to put your speech together utilizes all the information in the preceding chapters. If you are in doubt about the progression, review the chapter references indicated before you proceed to the next chapters on delivery and special speaking occasions.

7

DELIVERY METHODS AND SYSTEMS

The SEE factor:
Spontaneity
Enthusiasm
Eye Contact

Good delivery, like beauty, is in the eye of the beholder. For you, the speaker, this means your audience. How you look and sound to the audience will determine their response. Even if the content of your speech is exceptional, it can be lost on your audience through poor delivery. This chapter will deal with different ways to deliver your speech, and how you can make these methods work for you.

Your effectiveness as a speaker will depend on three elements of speech delivery: your spontaneity, your enthusiasm, and your eye contact. I call these the SEE factor, and all have a powerful effect on your audience. Anything that enhances your SEE factor enhances your impact on your audience. And, by the same token, anything that lessens your SEE factor lessens your impact on the audience. Here's why these elements are so essential to good delivery.

Spontaneity in your delivery makes everything you say sound like conversation—fresh, lively, interesting, made up on the spot just for this particular audience. Spontaneity is the opposite of just droning along as though you were parroting someone else's ideas. The big trick, of course, is to make your carefully prepared, well-organized speech sound spontaneous. This requires total mastery of the content of your speech, so that you are free to vary your ways of expressing your ideas to suit the audience.

Enthusiasm for your subject is absolutely essential to effective delivery. Enthusiasm is contagious. Your audience will listen and remember what you say if your attitude convinces them that you believe in your subject. If you are naturally a low-key person, you will have to work harder to display your enthusiasm. Remind yourself that your speech is your gift to this audience; it should be delivered with style and panache.

Eye contact enables your audience to establish a rapport with you as a person. It communicates your spontaneity and your enthusiasm; it turns what you are saying into a conversation and, thus, helps your audience concentrate on your message. Eye contact not only rivets attention on you, but it also instills confidence in you as a speaker. We consider people who won't look us in the eye when they speak as shifty, evasive, even deceitful. Unjust as that impression may be, it is universally believed, and the speaker should avoid such judgments by establishing eye contact quickly and maintaining it throughout the speech. Whatever lessens eye contact can be a severe handicap.

DELIVERY METHODS

All the elements of the SEE factor (Spontaneity, Enthusiasm, Eye Contact) are absolutely essential to good delivery, and should be considered when you evaluate the following standard methods of speech delivery.

Memorizing Your Entire Speech

This is a no-no for everyone but seasoned actors or those rare birds with photographic memories. For all the rest of us, it's a disaster. Memorized speeches sound canned and mechanical. Memorizing is dangerous, too, because the slightest distraction could sabotage your memory. Furthermore, it destroys spontaneity and enthusiasm, since you are so bent on remembering every word that the fire goes out of what may have been exciting concepts. Having your speech memorized might free you up to concentrate on making eye contact, but if you happen to look at someone who is stifling a yawn, your memory could forsake you. Therefore, the SEE factor for memorized speeches is right around zero.

Reading Your Entire Speech from a Manuscript

This is surely one of the worst ways to deliver a speech, especially for novice speakers. There is really no reason to do it unless you have no other choice, as, for instance, if you are to testify at a congressional committee hearing or other official hearing where every word will appear in permanent form in an official record, or if you have been asked to deliver a paper at a scientific or educational conference and every word will appear in a conference journal. In these instances, read your speech only if you are required to read it word for word. If you have a choice, don't read it. (I recommend you convert even a scientific paper into a speech rather than just reading it.) Reading from a manuscript to an audience expecting a speech destroys spontaneity and enthusiasm. And, of course, eye contact is almost impossible when your eyes are glued to the page. The SEE factor for reading your whole speech is also right around zero.

Impromptu

This method implies that you have had little or no time to prepare in advance. It is a method not so much decided upon as dictated by circumstance. You might be at a meeting and someone asks your opinion, or you might be at a political rally and want to contribute to the dialogue. These situations require being able to think on your feet about the subject being discussed. You are drawing only from your own knowledge because you have no time to do other kinds of research. This is the most common form of public speaking, so much so that we hardly think of it as a method of delivery. Yet it is part of many formal speeches. Question and Answer periods are impromptu, and are often the most exciting part of a presentation. The impromptu speech is characterized by spontaneity, enthusiasm, and maximum eye contact, and so has a very high SEE factor.

Extemporaneous

Extemporaneous is the style most used by speakers. The extemporaneous speech is prepared in advance, well organized, fully developed, carefully rehearsed, and delivered with the aid of an outline or notes, a manuscript with key ideas highlighted, or other aids. It gives you the security of having a written structure, yet allows you to look and sound spontaneous, to express enthusiasm for your subject, and to maintain eye contact. In short, its SEE factor is very high.

Another plus for the extemporaneous method is its flexibility; it allows you to use a combination of the other methods within your speech. For example, you can memorize a short quotation for your introduction or conclusion; you can read the testimony of an expert to shore up body points; and there are opportunities for impromptu remarks during the speech as well as in the Question and Answer period. If something suddenly pops into your mind that would add to your message, say it—impromptu remarks add spontaneity to any speech.

SYSTEMS OF DELIVERY

Systems of delivery are really road maps to show you where you are, and where you are going. You decide which system will help most, or perhaps, more important, which will hinder your delivery least. The system that offers you maximum freedom, and a measure of security in being able to remember what you want to say, will instill confidence and will be the right one for you. You have several choices. You can use the full text of your speech; you can prepare a detailed or a skeleton outline; you can use the Snyder Four-Card System; you can draw one big picture to visualize your whole speech; you can create a mental picture to be your guide; and, of course, you can combine some of these or create some mind-joggers of your own. The following explanations of these systems will help you decide which would be the most effective one for you.

Full Text

For some speakers, having the full text on the lectern acts like a security blanket. Unfortunately, the temptation is to start reading it, which, as I have said, is one of the worst ways to deliver a speech. Instead, know your speech thoroughly by rehearsing it several times, so you absorb its content. And follow the suggestions for highlighting it that I give later on in this chapter.

Detailed Outline

Every idea and every supporting idea is expressed in a complete sentence in a detailed outline. The relative importance of your ideas is expressed by roman numerals, capital letters, arabic numerals, and small letters. For example, here's a detailed outline of Point 1 in the body of the PAR speech we worked on in the previous chapter.

I. PAR will help you explain to an interviewer what you can do for the company.
   A. PAR will enable you to identify a Problem you have encountered.
   B. PAR will enable you to describe the Action you took to solve the problem.
   C. PAR will enable you to explain the Results.

A detailed outline is about one third the length of a full text, but that still means a lot of words to look at and absorb while you are trying to maintain eye contact. Rather than depending on words, teach yourself to think in terms of ideas. So if you're using a personal experience in the body of your speech, don't even write it out. Simply use an idea-jogger, like "College kids to help with survey." Then describe the experience in your own freshly spun words.

Skeleton Outline

Key ideas are expressed with a minimum of words in a skeleton outline. So the detailed outline above would be reduced to

How PAR works with interviewer:
    identifies problem
    describes action
    explains results

If you have written your speech out in full, and have rehearsed it until you know its content thoroughly, these key words should bring it all back to you at a glance, letting you maintain maximum eye contact and spontaneity.

Structure Notes

You can use the notations you made in structuring your speech as speech notes—that is, the index cards of the Snyder Four-Card System. To do this, you would reduce the three main points of the body of the PAR speech to three short sentences:

How PAR works.
How to write a PAR.
How to use PAR in job interviews.

This way, your entire speech could be noted on just three cards—the introduction, body, and conclusion. To rely only on index cards with confidence, however, you must of course know your speech very well; you must have rehearsed and rehearsed until you have thoroughly absorbed its content and need only the structure to recall it. Such minimal notes are ideal in that they allow for maximum eye contact and free you to show your enthusiasm for your subject in a spontaneous manner.

Pictures

This method entails actually visualizing your speech in picture form and drawing the picture on a large card—at least the size of a laundry shirt cardboard, or 12″ x 18″. The picture is your only "note." You do not need artistic talent to use this technique, but you do need an ability to turn concepts into meaningful images that will jog your memory. Obviously, as speaker, you must have written out a full speech and learned its content thoroughly before attempting to draw any images. Advocates of the pictures system say that the act of visualizing the speech is in itself a mind-jogger, and that eventually you will retain the image without even having to look at the picture you have drawn.

Mental Pictures

This system is also called stacking and linking. It conceives of a speech as a series of images stacked, one upon the other, like an acrobat's inverted pyramid. All must be linked together; the more absurdly, the better. In the PAR speech, for example, you might visualize a worried golfer in a sand trap, which would indicate your allusion to PAR in the introduction, as well as the fact that she has a problem that must be solved—how to make PAR. That image alone has put you into the body of your speech, since PAR is an acronym for Problem, Action, Result. You now add three thought-balloons coming out of her head. One shows Action—driving the golf ball and smiling; the second balloon shows Results —getting a loving cup with PAR engraved on it from a man wearing a hat that has "Boss" printed on it; the third balloon also shows Results—a check emerging from the loving cup. Your conclusion is a restatement, so you don't need an extra image for that.

Both the picture and the mental picture systems assume complete mastery of the content of your speech, so that you only need a simple guide to mark the progression of ideas. And both require much practice to be effective. Once mastered, they will give you the ultimate SEE factor.

The first four delivery systems (full text, detailed outline, skeleton outline, and structure notes) require that you use either cue cards or manuscripts at the lectern. Speaking from substantial notes may sound simple, but there are some tricks of the trade you should be aware of that will help you get the most out of your notes.

Cue cards

Cue cards are preferable to paper because they are easier to handle, more durable, and do not make distracting shuffling noises. Use large file cards, 5" x 7", 6" x 8", or even 8" by 10", so you have ample room for your cues. Number each card clearly and print your notations in large capital letters so you can read them easily at arm's length. If you have access to a speech typewriter, or any large-type typewriter, type your cards. Leave plenty of space between the lines and keep wide margins. Remember, you want to be able to see the notes at a glance; if you print too small, or the lines are too close together, you will lose eye contact. Wide spacing also gives you room to highlight ideas.

Flip charts, slides, overhead projections

Flip charts, slides, and overhead projections help you remember your points and also help your audience by offering a visual outline for everyone to refer to as you flesh out the key points your audience's attention is focused on.

Manuscripts

If you prefer to take the full text of your speech to the lectern, you should use standard-size typing paper, because the full text would require too many cards. If you do this, be sure that you type the speech especially for use at the lectern. If you have a large-type typewriter, use it. If not, use all caps on your regular typewriter, triple space, and leave wide margins. You must be able to refer to your manuscript at a glance. You are *not* going to read it (remember the SEE factor!), you are just going to refer to it, and you must be able to find your place quickly. Mark the salient points by underlining or boxing them. Number your pages to avoid mix-ups. To make sure your papers are neat and secure, use a loose-leaf binder or something to hold your pages neatly together; dropped pages are a disaster for a speaker.

Whether you use a manuscript or cue cards, you will be marking them up in the same manner. Use felt-tip pens of various colors for underlining and for indicating the relative importance of your points. For example, you might use red for major body points and blue for quotations or statistics and other specifics. You might draw a rectangle around certain key ideas. Use your margin for reminders, too. A black V can indicate a visual aid, or a check mark can show the end of the natural divisions in your speech—for example, the introduction, body points, and so on. Invent a system you will understand. All systems are directions on your road map; they will tell you where you are and where you are going.

I have tried to stress in this chapter that you should carefully choose your speech delivery method and system with your audience in mind. If your choice of method or system will allow you to present your speech in a spontaneous way, and enable you to get your enthusiasm for your subject across while maintaining maximum eye contact, you can be confident that your audience will respond with the appreciation your speech deserves.

8

VISUAL AIDS

There is only one ironclad rule about visual aids—if you can do without them, do without them. If the visual aid will make your point faster or better, by all means use it. But if it does not edify, clarify, enhance, or dramatize what you are saying, it may be more bother than it's worth. Most speeches do not need visual aids.

In a recent poll, communications experts were asked to name the speeches they considered to be the most memorable. The top three on the list used no visual aids: Lincoln's Gettysburg address; Churchill's maiden speech as prime minister, "I have nothing to offer but blood, toil, tears, and sweat"; and Martin Luther King's speech at the Lincoln Memorial civil rights rally, "I have a dream . . ."

There are times, of course, when a visual aid is almost the only way you can get a point across without a barrage of words. Suppose, for example, that you are a financial expert talking to lay people about investments. You want to use the term "tombstone" to describe the kind of advertisement, usually found in the financial section of a newspaper, that offers stock for sale. A visual aid would reinforce your description in this case far better than words alone, so use it.

Whatever simplifies, reinforces, or makes your speech more vivid can be considered a necessary visual aid.

But if you do decide that a visual aid is needed for the clarification or enhancement of your presentation, there are a few general guidelines that you should follow to maximize the success of both your visual aid and your speech.

Visibility

A visual aid must be visible to your whole audience or it is worse than useless. A visual aid that can't be seen negates the whole purpose of a visual aid. To prevent such visibility problems, you must know in advance how many people will be in your audience, the size of the room, and the type of lighting. Check out your aid in that room beforehand so that you know it can be seen by everyone. If the audience is small (up to fifteen people) and your visual aid is a chart, it needn't be the size of a billboard to be seen. On the other hand, if your audience is large and scattered across a large auditorium, you will have to put your chart on a slide and project it if your audience is to see it.

Speaker's Spotlight

If you are going to show a slide, videotape, or film in a darkened room, be sure that you, the speaker, are not in the dark. You are a living visual aid, the most important one; you must not be upstaged by whatever other aid you are using. You can prevent this by arranging for a small light to shine on you so your voice is not disembodied. You must remain visible to retain your authority.

Speaker's Place

If your visual aid is a chart or graph propped on an easel, stand beside it and point out what you want the audience to focus upon. But when you speak, speak to the audience, not to the chart. Using a pointer is helpful; you will not have to lean into the chart or risk obscuring what you are trying to display.

If you are using an overhead projector, use a pointer and indicate on the screen whatever you want the audience to focus on. Do not point to the acetate sheet on the light box, for it will just distract your audience.

Visual Rehearsal

Visual aids must be integrated into your script or outline or notes, and rehearsed exactly as you intend to present them in your speech. Even if your visual aid is just one word on a card that you are going to hold up and put right down again, you must rehearse with it exactly as you intend to deliver it to your audience. You need to be able to handle your visual aids with aplomb. No fumbling allowed.

Timing

Do not show your visual aid until you are ready to talk about it. As soon as you have finished talking about it, put it away—out of sight. Otherwise, your audience will keep looking at it, and you will lose their attention.

KINDS OF VISUAL AIDS

Any pictorial presentation of an idea is a visual aid. This includes charts, graphs, diagrams, chalkboards, flannel boards, film or tape clips, slides, and objects. All visual aids fall into three categories—direct, projected, and dynamic—and all have special requirements for speaker and audience.

Direct Visual Aids

Direct visuals are the simplest and most common aids. These include all manner of charts and graphs, flannel boards and chalkboards, pictures, objects, and even people or animals used as models.

It is easy to make a **word chart** effective. Be sure to

> Keep it simple
> No more than four lines
> Make key points only
> Print large, with all caps

The word chart is a handy way to explain an acronym. For example, if you want your audience to remember the origin of POSH, you can explain that it was a term used by British travel agents booking passage for VIPS going to India. POSH indicated that their staterooms were to be on the port side going out to India and on the starboard side coming home to England, to afford them the best breezes and comforts going and coming. A word chart would do it quickly:

```
POSH
PORT
OUT
STARBOARD
HOME
```

Flannel boards are especially effective if you have data that change, because you can substitute one element for another simply by picking it off the flannel board and putting on the new element. However, this does take preplanning and preparation. The flannel board itself is simple enough to make. Use a 2' x 4' piece of plywood (or fiberboard or Masonite) and cover it with a tightly drawn piece of flannel. Then prepare your visuals—cut them out of good-quality drawing paper and paste pieces of rough sandpaper on the back of each. The sandpaper will adhere to the flannel board and can easily be lifted off and replaced. This device has the advantage of allowing the speaker to retain maximum eye contact with the audience while being able to illustrate a point in a clever manner. It also allows for quick removal of the visual when the point has been made.

Chalkboards are also handy, but they require that you turn your back to the audience when you are chalking up your data. Remember, do not speak to the board; wait till you have finished writing, and then speak to the audience. And, when possible, prepare the board in advance. Writing while talking is a drawback, unless you are very fast and write or draw very clearly.

Drawing figures does not require artistic talent. Once you get the hang of using circles, triangles, rectangles, and straight lines to construct a figure, you will be able to illustrate any action with a quick sketch or prepare simple pictographs. Draw your figure in pencil on lined paper first, to get the proportions right. Then darken the lines with a heavy marker, and trace the figure onto a presentable sheet of plain paper.

Visual Aids • 81

Basic female figure

You can distinguish the basic male figure from the female figure by making the body rectangular.

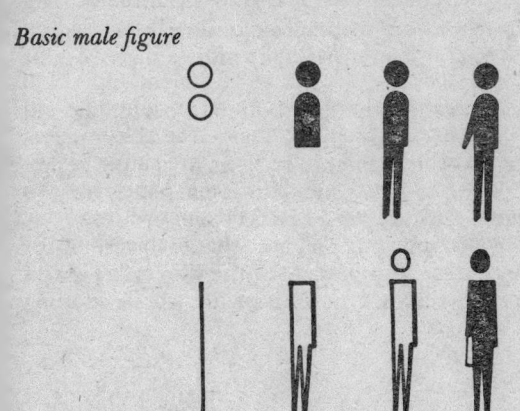

Basic male figure

Note that body and legs are of equal length.

Charts are "graphic statistics" and should be made to be seen at a glance. More complex data, if they are necessary to explain your subject, should be handed out after your talk rather than shown as visual aids during your speech. Here are some examples of simple charts that are good visual aids if they are made big enough and clear enough to be seen by all.

Pictograph chart

PERCENTAGE OF WORKERS HOLDING TWO OR MORE JOBS

Source: Department of Labor - 1974

Using figures to show percentages has more of an impact than words alone, and is more visually interesting than line or bar graphs.

When you want to show the distribution of percentages of the whole, you can use a **pie chart.** The circle or pie represents the whole and the segments or slices of the pie represent the parts. The pie is a wonderful visual aid as long as the smallest segment can be seen by everyone.

As a guide for plotting your pie, note that each slice of the following circle represents 5 percent of the whole; the marks within each slice represent 1 percent of the whole. Plotting figures are cumulative.

Visual Aids • 83

Pie Charts

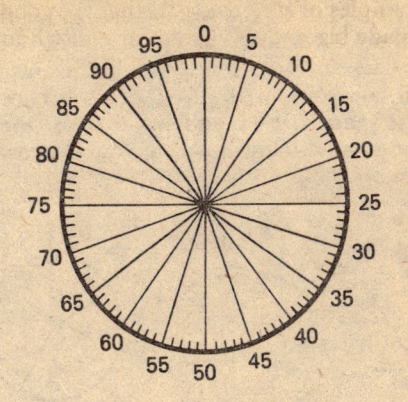

Using this model as your plotting scale, you can make a pie chart of anything that uses percentages. For instance, if you are giving a talk on energy and you want to show who uses energy, you could express it in a pie chart:

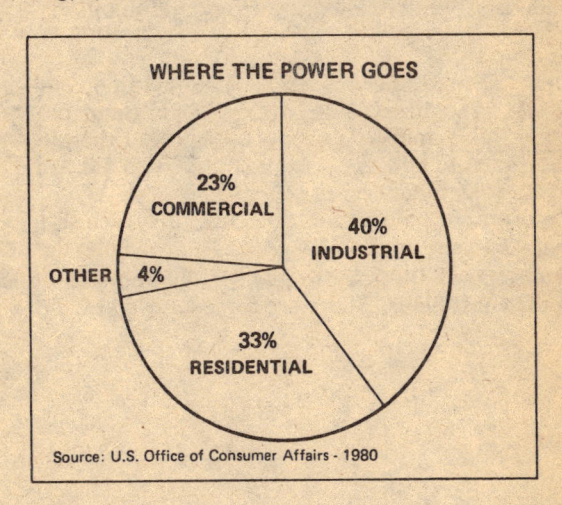

WHERE THE POWER GOES

- 23% COMMERCIAL
- 40% INDUSTRIAL
- OTHER 4%
- 33% RESIDENTIAL

Source: U.S. Office of Consumer Affairs - 1980

Coloring the segments you want to highlight will add to the

84 • SPEAK FOR YOURSELF WITH CONFIDENCE

visibility of your aid and dramatize your point. Be sure that your segments add up to the whole pie—100 percent.

The size of the circle can change to represent an increase or decrease between time segments. For example, suppose you want to compare medical expenses for an American family for the years '80, '81, and '82. Increase the size of the circles to indicate visually how medical expenses have increased annually.

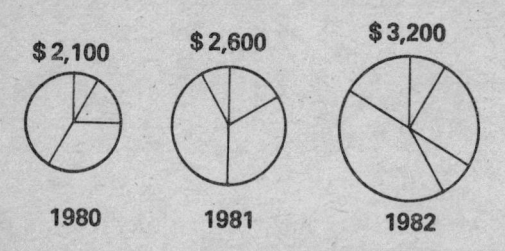

$2,100 $2,600 $3,200

1980   1981   1982

The segments would indicate what percentage of the whole was spent for various kinds of health care: insurance, doctors, dentists, ophthalmologists, drugs, and so on.

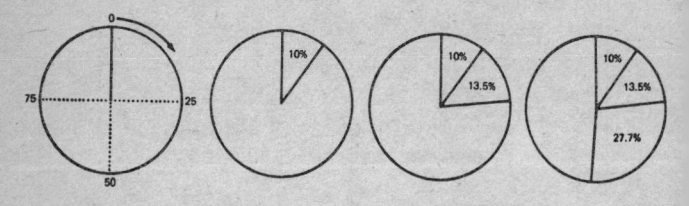

Bar charts will be easier to make if you know how to construct the chart fields. There are three basic types:

Visual Aids • 85

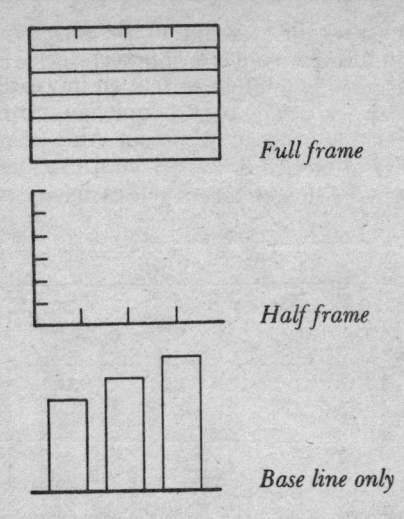

Full frame

Half frame

Base line only

Curve or **line charts** are effective for showing a rise or fall, an increase or decrease, over a period of time. For example, the chart below shows the rise of the number of women in the labor force over a period of thirty years, and the slight decline of men during the same time.

Curve charts

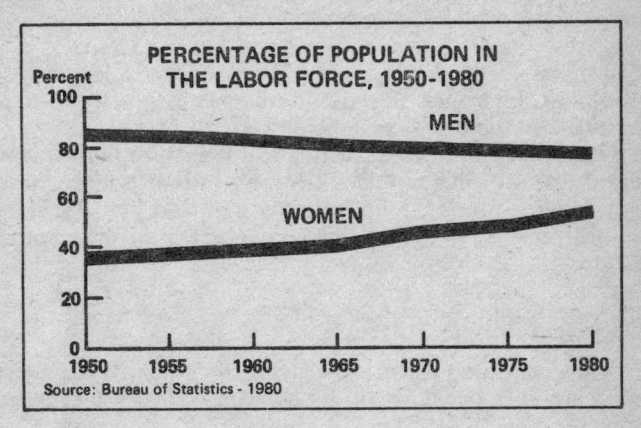

PERCENTAGE OF POPULATION IN THE LABOR FORCE, 1950-1980

MEN

WOMEN

Source: Bureau of Statistics - 1980

Use different-colored markers for each line so the lines will be readily seen and distinguished from one another. And, of course, be sure the chart is big enough to be seen by all.

Bar charts or **graphs** are especially useful for comparing events or ideas that are easily grasped at a glance. For example, the life expectancy of men and women from 1900 to 1970 is expressed with great visual impact in this bar chart:

Bar charts

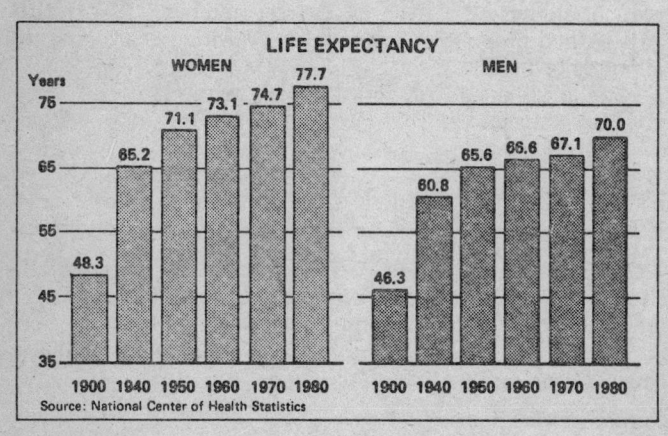

LIFE EXPECTANCY

Years	WOMEN						MEN					
	1900	1940	1950	1960	1970	1980	1900	1940	1950	1960	1970	1980
	48.3	65.2	71.1	73.1	74.7	77.7	46.3	60.8	65.6	66.6	67.1	70.0

Source: National Center of Health Statistics

(Source: Bureau of Labor Statistics, 1975)

Bar charts need color to stand out as visual aids. Use strong primary colors, such as red and blue, to heighten the contrast. Ink in the numbers in bold black.

If your audience is small (up to fifteen people), poster-size charts are adequate. But if your audience is large, have your charts prepared on 35mm slides and project them on a screen, so that they are clearly visible to your entire group.

Displaying objects

Whatever object you are displaying or demonstrating must be clearly seen by all. If you are showing a small sculpture to

Visual Aids • 87

a handful of people around a table, the work of art may be worth a thousand words about the expertise of the artist. However, showing the same piece to five hundred people in a huge hall will mean frustration for one and all.

In addition to ensuring an aid's visibility, you must see that it is displayed to its best advantage. Don't hold it in front of you; prop it up someplace or hold it at arm's length so all can focus on the object rather than on your dress or suit. If you are going to talk about parts of an object, again, each part should be visible to all. If it isn't, you'd be better off with an enlarged photo, slide, acetate, or drawing—with separate visuals showing each part.

Handle all props with great care, as though they were expensive objects. Your attitude as revealed in your gestures toward them will determine how your audience will respond. If your audience is small, you can walk around and show the object to each audience member individually. But don't hand it to someone and suggest he pass it along; if you do that, no one will hear a word you say until your prop is back in your hands.

As with all other visual aids, be sure that you rehearse with the object so that you handle it naturally.

Projected Visual Aids

If you have an audience of more than thirty people, most objects, charts, and graphs will not be easily visible to everyone at once. If the visuals are important to your speech, you would be wise to project them onto a screen—either with slides, or with transparancies on an overhead projector—so that everyone can see them. Another advantage to projected images, besides the visibility, is that you can stop showing the aid as soon as you have finished talking about it, so the audience does not continue to gaze at it while you move on to another point.

There are also some dangers that go along with using projected visuals. There is a tendency to use more visuals than you need, because you have gone to the trouble of preparing slides or transparencies. Keep in mind that a speech that relies too heavily on projected images is really not a speech at all—it's a voice-over narration.

The cardinal rule of using **slides** in a speech is to rehearse, with the projector and slides and screen, *exactly* what you plan to do in your presentation. Keep rehearsing until you feel comfortable. If possible, it is best to rehearse in the room where you will be speaking, with the projector and screen where they will actually be during your speech. Be sure that everyone has a clear view of the screen and of you. Remember that you are the most important visual aid, and should not be reduced to a disembodied voice in the dark. Even if the auditorium must be dark, you need a small light to illuminate you. Mark your script, outline, or notes so you know exactly when to show your slides.

When preparing your slides, keep these guidelines in mind:

- Convey one idea per slide.
- Limit the words on your slide to around fifteen.
- Make lettering legible.
- Keep subject content simple.
- Use color whenever you can—in photos and graphic illustrations.
- Use several slides to explain complicated material.

And remember to check the equipment an hour or so before you are scheduled to speak, to be sure everything is as it should be. You must:

- See to it that the projector is plugged in.
- Have enough extension cord to run the projector safely. If it is a long cord, tape it to the floor and put up a "Be Careful of Extension Cord" sign.
- Make sure you have the correct plug or adapter.
- Run two or three slides to see that your slides are advancing properly. Then return tray to starting position.

Visual Aids • 89

- Cue whoever will assist you so they know when to turn lights off and on.
- Check to see that the room is dark enough when you turn the lights off; good slide viewing depends on darkness.
- Check your small speaker's light to be sure it does not interfere with the projected image. If it does, get a light that doesn't.

The **overhead projector** is one of the most versatile and effective of visual aid tools, and has several advantages over the slide projector. With an overhead projector, you can run your own projector from the front of the room, and you can keep all the lights on while using it. These are invaluable advantages for a speaker, since they enable you to control the visuals at all times, and to maintain your eye contact with a visible audience.

In addition, you can create your own visuals right in front of your audience, because the transparencies can be marked with a grease pencil or any number of colorful special transparency pens. This allows you to create instant charts, figures, or drawings as you would on a chalkboard, which adds to the spontaneity of your presentation.

You can project many things in many ways on an overhead projector, such as:

- Basic transparencies, which you can photocopy beforehand and hand out after your presentation.
- Text and photographs from books, magazines, newspapers, and other sources.
- Object silhouettes.
- A small part of a transparency at a time, using the gradual disclosure technique.
- Tinted transparencies, which can be used to add interest and realism, to emphasize a main point, or to color-code your show as a quick reminder of what's coming up next.

Overhead projectors are ideal for small meetings and training modules, demonstrations, and presentations in a classroom or small conference room. Much of what has been said about slide presentation is also true of transparencies for overhead projection. However, there are a few considerations that are unique to the overhead projector:

- Pay special attention to the projector's lamp. Turn it off as soon as your audience has studied the visual you are talking about, otherwise they may continue to pay attention to it instead of to you. If you have several transparencies to show and there is some time between them in your speech, turn off the light and turn it on again when needed. Or, use an opaque acetate sheet to block the light.
- In rehearsal, be especially mindful of the temptation to look at the light table right in front of you instead of at the screen where the image is being projected. If you want the audience to focus on the screen, you too must focus on the screen. If you want to point to some part of your visual, don't do it on the acetate; point to the image on the screen.
- If you use the same acetates frequently, mount them on cardboard frames. They will be easier to handle.
- Use horizontal formats whenever possible to maximize visibility.

Dynamic Visual Aids

Any visual system that incorporates motion and sound is called a dynamic visual. The most commonly used ones are film and videotape.

When you use **film** or **tape** as part of your presentation, be sure that you have it racked up and ready to roll as soon as you need it. Nothing is more annoying than sitting around waiting while someone threads the machine and adjusts the volume and focus. That kind of fiddling will turn off even the most eager audience. So check before the meeting, and be sure everything is in perfect working order. If your entire presentation is on film or tape, be sure that your narration is properly keyed. Also make certain that there is a small light on you, so you retain your authority as the presenter of the

Visual Aids • 91

film/tape. An hour before your presentation, be sure to check the location of your projector and screen, so you know your audience can see the screen clearly. Also check your lighting cues, so that whoever is assisting you will turn lights on and off at the right time. (Review the other check procedures for slides, which also apply to film/tape, on pages 88–89.)

The film/tape should support the subject and purpose of your speech. Make sure that your introduction tells your audience what you are going to focus on, and that your narration reminds the audience of points pertinent to your speech statement being made by the film.

Remember that most speeches do not need visual aids. If you can do without them, then do. They should be used only if they will further your speech—if they clarify, enhance, or dramatize a point you want to make.

BODY LANGUAGE

9

Body language is nonverbal communication. Without saying a word, you tell your audience something about your attitude and feelings through your posture, gestures, facial expression, and movements, especially eye contact. If you are not conscious of this subtle power of body language, your verbal delivery can clash with your nonverbal message, which undermines the strength of your speech.

As a speaker, you must become aware of your own body language so that you communicate positive messages both nonverbally and verbally. The ideal way to do this, of course, is to watch yourself on videotape as you rehearse a speech. Lacking that equipment, you can rehearse in front of a full-length mirror or get a friend to critique your rehearsal. However you do it, regard this step as an essential part of your preparation, because it is crucial to delivering an effective speech, a speech that will elicit the response from your audience that you want them to have.

Though body language as it applies to speakers is a comparatively new science known as kinesics, we are all aware of it in our daily lives, and actually judge people based on their physical behavior. Take shaking hands, for instance. We think of a firm handshake as a mark of good character and of a limp one as indicative of indecision or weakness. The recipient of the weak handshake also can feel vaguely insulted, as though the limp hand indicates condescension or dismissal.

Eye contact evokes even more comment than the handshake. If people don't look at us, we mark them as shifty. On the other hand, if they stare, we think them rude.

Your own personal experiences with the body language of friends or family will help you to understand its importance to you as a speaker. Movements that you find distracting in others will be distracting to an audience: grimacing; pulling your ear; toying with your hair or fiddling with notes, glasses, the microphone; slumping on the lectern; grasping the lectern in a viselike grip; shifting from foot to foot; gesturing wildly; pacing about aimlessly; gaping at the ceiling; staring at the floor; adjusting your clothing; scratching; tapping your foot; shuffling; and so on. Become aware of these random movements before your presentation. Most of them are caused by lack of confidence, which can be overcome by diligent attention to all phases of speech preparation and rehearsal. Practice the appropriate body language as you rehearse. As you become more and more confident about what you are going to say and how you are going to say it, your gestures will become a natural part of your speech. But remember, good speech planning is the road to confidence.

Since you have already prepared your speech with great care, you are now ready for a dress rehearsal. Set the scene for your body language exercise. Sit in a chair as if you were on stage and about to be introduced. Sit erect, yet not stiff. Every eye in the audience will be on you. Your posture speaks before you open your mouth. So you've got to look the part of the featured speaker, keeping in mind the powerful nonverbal impact you're sending to your audience. They will form their first impression of you based on body language alone—in just five to ten seconds. First impressions are the basis of attitudes, and are hard to change. And remember, first impressions are based on body language alone.

Spend some time looking in a mirror (or have a videotape made), to find a posture, a presence, that speaks positively about you. Good posture not only looks good; it's also good for voice production and good for your confidence. Sit up straight in a confident, relaxed way. Try crossing your ankles. How does that look? How does it feel? Experiment. Try crossing your knees. If it looks good and feels good, fine. Do not, however, jerk your foot up and down from the crossed knee. Any distracting visible body action works against you by becoming a negative focal point for your audience. Wiggle your toes in your shoes instead. That will give you a physical outlet for nervousness (just as jerking your foot would), but no one can see you wiggling your toes.

Try sitting in a two-L position. That's when your torso (back against the back of your chair) and upper legs form the first L, and you form the second L by letting your feet sit flat on the floor. Again, experiment. If you feel comfortable, you will look comfortable. Seek that state of being.

Plan where you will look when your host is at the lectern introducing you. Toward the lectern or at your audience? What facial expression is appropriate when the audience is looking at you and listening to the flattering remarks your host is making about you? This can be an embarrassing moment if you don't anticipate it, especially if the host embellishes your credentials and flatters you unexpectedly. Whatever happens, whether you are simply welcomed or lavishly lauded, the best response is an honest one, but temper it. Look toward the host, and listen to what is being said in case you want to allude to it once you begin speaking. (Such an acknowledgment of your host's remarks would precede the introduction of your speech.)

Your facial expression when all eyes are on you and forming their first impressions should be subdued, limited, controlled, objective—a small enigmatic or thoughtful smile will look and feel right. At this point especially, you'll want control of your body language. Firm control of your nonverbal communication will help you handle your prespeech jitters, simply because you will be concentrating on doing something you know you do well.

While you're listening to the host's introduction (it will only take a minute or two at most), you should also be nonchalantly and unobtrusively taking several deep breaths through your nose. Breathe in deeply, as though you were smelling your favorite flower, then exhale through your mouth to relieve tension buildup. Do not inhale through your mouth—it will make your mouth feel dry. After this breathing warm-up, you will inhale normally during your speech, taking breaths as they are needed. You might have to pause to take needed breaths as you are speaking. Fine. You audience will wait patiently. You will be far more pleasant to listen to if you have the air you need to speak on instead of puffing like a steam engine. While you're doing these simple breathing exercises, you can also run over your opening sentence in your mind so you have it on the tip of your tongue.

There is one other thing you should be doing during your host's introduction: Notice how far your host is standing away from the microphone. If your host is six feet tall and you're only five feet, the microphone must be lowered or tilted to accommodate your size. If this isn't done for you, do it for yourself before you begin speaking. The microphone should be level with your chin.

When the host's introduction is over, the audience will applaud in anticipation. You will be waved to the speaker's stand by the host. Again, every eye will be on you. How are you going to rise out of your chair with dignity and grace at a moment like this? Getting out of a chair is a clumsy task, even when no one is watching, so practice this action during your speech rehearsal. Practice so that you can rise effortlessly from your chair, without stress or discomfort. You'll feel a lot better if you know how you look to others. Rehearse this in front of a mirror.

Next, you're going to have to move from the chair to your speaking position. Rehearse this. Stand tall. Walk gracefully. Look out for obstacles—wires, chairs, whatever—but don't stare at your feet. Walk confidently, sending out messages with your body language. Experiment to find the signals that say what your nonverbal message should say—warmth. How can you get your body to say, "I'm glad to see all of you here today"? A smile will do it, for starters. Send an enthusiastic signal that says "I'm delighted to be here today." Let your audience know you're comfortable. Find a posture or movement that conveys confidence. A few run-throughs at home in front of a mirror will help you find the right body signals and so give you more confidence.

The next step is moving into your speaking position. The following criteria for lectern behavior will make getting into position simple. (If there is no lectern, you should rehearse with that fact in mind, and make the necessary adjustments.) These instructions, with practice, should enable you to place yourself quickly and confidently on the speaking platform so that you are comfortable and ready to speak:

> First, stand six to eight inches *behind* the lectern. Stand tall. Adjust the microphone, if necessary. Place your notes (or manuscript or outline) on top of the lectern and leave them there; don't fuss with them. (When you get to the spoken-language part of your stand-up rehearsal, practice handling your notes unobtrusively. Naturally, you will not read your notes—you will just refer to them. So rehearse speaking with your head up, your eyes looking out at the audience.)

These instructions sound simple, but maintaining total control over your body—from your feet on up—is surprisingly difficult. If you are speaking at a lectern and there's a stationary mike at that lectern, you cannot move from that spot if your audience is to hear you clearly. You should stand solidly on both feet and stay there. Plant your feet. Root yourself like a tree. Center yourself. Once you get into the habit of standing tall and rooted, you will be in control of your whole body, and your audience will get a body language message that says you are in control. The speaker who is not in control, who constantly shifts his weight from foot to foot, looks sloppy and too casual. The speaker who is not in control crosses his feet, loses his balance, and risks falling. The speaker who does not stand rooted on both feet sways and tends to do little nervous dance steps, which distract the audience. So, stand tall and stand still. It isn't easy, but if you practice it during your rehearsals it will help you to be a better speaker.

What are you going to do with your hands? Think about it. Experiment. Find out what is comfortable for you during your home rehearsal, not in front of your audience. You can hold on to the lectern; the sides are a very reassuring place to rest your hands. Don't hold on so tightly that your knuckles pale from the life-or-death clutch, just grasp the lectern edges gently. Holding onto the midsection of the lectern top will, in most cases, cause you to tense your mid-arms, which in turn will cause you to tense the rest of your body. Avoid this. Also, holding onto the topmost section of the lectern top will bring you physically too close to your audience, as well as too close to the lectern itself; remember to stand six to eight inches behind it at all times. You can have your hands hanging comfortably at your sides; or have one hand in your pocket (with the other hand hanging down at your side or holding the edge of the lectern); or have both hands somehow folded in front of you.

So experiment, and find out what makes you comfortable and works for your needs. Your major consideration in placing your hands should be to have them free and available to use when a gesture will help your audience understand what you're talking about. For example, if you said, "She was a big woman," an accompanying gesture would immediately tell your audience what you meant—fat? tall? big in character? Such gestures (as long as they are not wild to the point of distraction) can only help your speech; not only do they help your listeners understand, but gestures also help you to release excess energy, which will make you feel more at ease.

During this body language rehearsal, give yourself a pep talk. Tell yourself that you're going to enjoy giving this speech. Tell yourself that you're going to have fun. Tell yourself that you're going to enjoy your audience. In time, these messages become a self-fulfilling prophecy. So talk to yourself. Tell yourself you're terrific. Tell yourself this is a wonderful life experience for you, and you're going to do it with confidence and style. Psyching yourself up is an important part of your speech preparation.

As I have mentioned, the most important nonverbal tool you have is eye contact. Eye contact entails looking into the eyes of your listeners 99 percent of the time. While you talk to them, you should be looking at them. When you are at the lectern, or speaking before any audience, you can effectively reach out to your listeners by looking at them, eye to eye.

98 • SPEAK FOR YOURSELF WITH CONFIDENCE

People notice when a speaker looks at them. They expect it; don't disappoint them. If your audience is small, you can establish eye contact with every person in the room by making a conscious effort to do so. Look at one person when you begin. Speak to and connect with that person briefly, then move on to someone else, as you do when you're conversing in an informal circle of friends. On and on. Your eye contact should be natural and relaxed. It should not be mechanical, jerky, or contrived; it should be an easy sweep of your eyes on theirs—not staring.

Your eye contact technique will differ slightly with a larger audience. Again, you will use a gentle, easy sweep of your eyes across theirs, but you will not be able to connect with everyone in the hall. To give your audience the feeling that you are reaching out to all of them, try using the "Z sweep." To do this, use the letter Z like a road map for your eye contact sweep; move your eyes in a line following the contour of a giant letter Z.

It's always a good idea to use eye contact as feedback, too. This will build your confidence while you're building bridges to your audience. To use eye contact feedback, favor the individuals who seem entranced, sympathetic, in agreement with you, enjoying your presentation. Their positive body language will help you, if you take note of the supportive feelings being sent to you and allow them to make you feel good. Do not, whatever you do, dwell on or worry about or return your gaze to faces that send frowns, yawns, or looks of boredom. Ignore their negative messages by passing them gently by, and return and linger on your cheering section— the smilers, the sympathetic ones.

But always keep in mind just what eye contact means. It is not looking just above people's heads. It is not looking at the ceiling, the floor, or out the window. Eye contact is visual connection, particularly with receptive listeners. Speak to your audience with your eyes; this is the most powerful communication tool you have. Try it in your speech rehearsal. Try it when you're conversing with a colleague. Are you looking into the eyes of your conversation partner? Start honing your awareness in one-to-one situations, then take the technique out to every audience you face.

Finally, before you start to speak and put these body language tips into action, be sure your audience is ready for you to begin. Make sure they are quiet, attentive, and ready to listen. If they're not, wait. If the pause you take before starting does not quiet them, tactfully ask for silence, perhaps with a sentence like, "I'm ready when you are." Then greet them with a salutation that makes contact between you. A simple "Good morning" is sufficient. Or, "I'm happy to be here with you." Or, "Greetings, I'm glad you could make it." Or you can thank the host if your introduction was handled with special polish and style. Or say, "Hello everyone, I've been looking forward to this occasion. . . ." After that show of warmth, enthusiasm, confidence, and good feeling, pause and then start your speech.

To sum it all up, your verbal and nonverbal communication will give your audience the same message only if you have taken the trouble to prepare every aspect of your presentation from the moment you are in the view of your audience to the final applause at the end. Confidence, which comes with practice, is the key to controlling your body language.

REHEARSAL AND DELIVERY

10

Every speech you give is a stage performance starring you. How effective it will be will depend on both what you have to say and how you say it. You have a carefully prepared speech, after having followed the concepts detailed in the first nine chapters, but now you must concern yourself with how to deliver it to get the response you want from your audience. There is no shortcut to success; you must rehearse and rehearse and rehearse until you know your speech so well that just a glance at your notes will bring it to mind.

Rehearsal is not just one hurried run-through. You may need six, eight, or more full-dress rehearsals, using all your props, visual aids, and notes, to be really prepared. If you can rehearse at the site where you are to speak, that's ideal. If not, simulate the location as closely as you can. If you have access to video, and can look at yourself on videotape, that's a great plus. If not, ask a couple of friends to listen to you and give you feedback. If that is not feasible, do at least one rehearsal in front of a mirror, so you can observe your body language. Listen to the verbal part of your speech on a cassette so you can check your timing and pace and voice level. Do everything you can to boost your confidence so that on D day you will deliver it exactly the way you want to. Spread

Rehearsal and Delivery • 101

your rehearsals out over several days, or even a full week, saving the final run-through for the day of your engagement. Such an extended rehearsal schedule will help you to psyche yourself up for the performance even as you refine your delivery with each practice session.

Everything about making a speech is very personal, and will vary from speaker to speaker. The following suggestions are, therefore, not rules; they are only guidelines that have been followed by many successful speakers and may be helpful to you. Rehearsal is a necessity, but you must decide which is the best way for you to rehearse. How many rehearsals, and where and when, is up to you. Here are some tips that may be helpful:

- Review the checklists in Chapter 1 so that you know the facilities available to you (and you have ordered what you will need) and the makeup of your audience. Being famil-

Know the Seating Arrangement

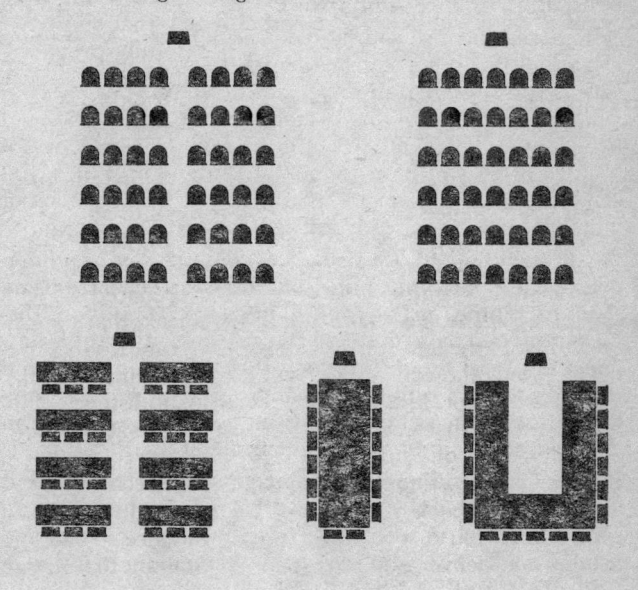

iar with where you will speak and to whom should be uppermost in your mind as you rehearse.

- As you rehearse, think about your audience sitting before you. Knowing the seating arrangement will help you consider appropriate body language and voice projection needs. This knowledge will also add to your confidence when you actually stand before your audience.
- Rehearse as though you were actually delivering your speech to an audience. Stand up and go through your speech from beginning to end, complete with natural gestures, visual aids, and your notes, outline, or manuscript.
- If, in rehearsal, you fluff a line or lose your place in your notes or mishandle a visual aid, keep right on going as though you were actually delivering your speech. Handle your mistake as well as you can, because goof-ups are human and may happen while you are making your real presentation. Cover your error as gracefully as possible, and remember Snyder's Law: "When the unexpected happens, don't agonize—improvise."
- With each rehearsal you should have to refer to your notes less and less. Do not shuffle them or fuss with them in any way as you speak because that cuts down on your eye contact, your most potent body language. In fact, you should be able to judge whether you need more rehearsal or not by how often you have to look at your notes. When you can just glance at them and then deliver a whole section of your speech, you're ready for your actual presentation.
- If you are going to use visual aids, be sure you have integrated them into your notes, and that you rehearse using them each time, just as you will in your presentation. Display them exactly as they will be presented, and know how you will reveal them, how long they will be in view, and how you will get rid of them when you have stopped talking about them. Remember, visual aids should not be in view either before or after you talk about them.
- Review Chapter 9 on body language, and keep in mind as you rehearse that your nonverbal communication can speak louder than words. Be sure that your gestures and actions match what you are saying. Remember that a well-

Rehearsal and Delivery • 103

placed smile does a warm-up job on your audience. A smile builds rapport, and makes you look wonderful.
- Always time your speech in rehearsal. An invitation to give a ten-minute speech means it must be timed to last ten minutes, and no more. The average speaker talks at an average rate of 125 to 160 words a minute, but if you are using visual aids and need time to display them, you cannot judge the time by words alone. So don't just read the words or count the words to decide on the timing; judge by the complete rehearsal time that includes movement, gestures, pauses, speaking, and handling visual aids.
- Rehearse your speech in front of friends, family, or colleagues to get a reading on both your content and manner. Ask for an overall view and then invite them to be picky, especially about any mannerisms in your delivery that distracted them from what you were saying. Ask them to tell you what your speech was about in a sentence. If your presentation was on target, they should almost repeat your speech statement. Ask if they were interested in the overall concept, and if they were bored with any particular aspects. Then, if you trust their judgment, make adjustments according to their comments.
- Rehearsing in front of a mirror can give you an idea of your posture and facial expressions, and can make you aware of glaring defects. It is not as good as a videotape of your rehearsal, of course, but if that is not available, your reflection will at least alert you to mannerisms that need to be changed. Most people are completely unaware of their mannerisms when speaking. Watch yourself.
- Record your rehearsal on a cassette recorder. Listening to the playback will be invaluable in pacing and timing your speech. It will show you when to speed up or slow down. It will help you improve your tone and style. A tape recorder is the speaker's best friend, so if you don't have one, borrow one.
- If there will be a Question and Answer period following your speech, rehearse that, too. Get one of your colleagues to ask questions that are relevant to your subject. Ideally, you should get someone who is representative of the real

audience you will face. For example, if you will be speaking to accountants, ask an accountant friend to pose questions that occur to her while you are speaking. Also, review Chapter 13, on the Question and Answer period.

- Your speech will be a little different every time you rehearse it. That's only natural since you are not reading it and you have not memorized it. The ideas you want to get across are the main thing; don't get hung up on particular ways of expressing those ideas. Chances are, the more familiar you are with the ideas, the better you will be able to express them as you continue to rehearse. Your speech will sound more and more conversational, and that's the ultimate aim of any speech—to sound like good conversation.

- Know your introduction and your conclusion well enough so that you do not have to refer to your notes. It is crucial to establish eye contact during your introduction and at the end of your speech. In the beginning, your eye contact establishes warmth, rapport, and confidence between you and the audience. At the end, your eye contact reinforces those emotional ties. Rehearse until you can deliver both these sections of your speech with ease, without dependence on notes.

WATCH YOUR DICTION

Another important reason to rehearse is to make sure that you are speaking clearly, that you enunciate every word distinctly. A cassette recording of your rehearsal can be a big help in this endeavor, for it will keep you from sliding into such sloppy pronunciation as, for example, "the Murrikin way of life." In other words, "Speak the speech, I prithee, trippingly on the tongue." If you have composed a sentence that tends to mush together—as "mares eat oats" so easily blurs into "mairsey doats," to give one instance—then rephrase the idea. If you tend to elide syllables, practice giving every syllable its due: A-mer-i-can. Good diction is important to a successful speech. If yours could stand improvement, perhaps the following suggestions will help:

- If you have a strong regional accent but are speaking outside of your own area, be careful to avoid using idioms that will not be understood, or pronunciations that are mystifying to your audience. For example, people from Pierre, South Dakota, will tell you they're from "Peer." Milwaukeans leave out the "l" so it sounds like they're from "M'waukee." I don't mean to say that your accent itself should be changed—most people find accents of other regions interesting and charming—but a speaker must be understood. If you can, it would be helpful to go over your speech with someone from the region where you will be speaking. The same holds true for those speakers with foreign accents. An Englishman extolling the virtues of "Mouzle," his favorite town in Cornwall, had better explain that it is spelled Mouse Hole if he expects us to find our way there. Don't worry about having an accent; worry about being understood.

- In general, pronounce proper nouns slowly and carefully—people's names, book titles, geographic locations. Repeat them to be sure people heard you correctly, especially if they are important to your speech. If you're talking about a book, hold it up and say the name of the author and its title, or project a slide blowup of the cover.

- When using acronyms, be sure your audience knows what the acronym stands for; for example, you would make certain they know NOW is the National Organization for Women. If you use initials for a well-known agency, be sure you give the agency's full name more than once, as with the SBA, which is the Small Business Administration. If in your speech you continually refer to initials or an acronym, it's a good idea to put the complete name before your audience on a chalkboard or flip chart, so they won't have to wonder again and again what the letters stand for.

- Foreign words and phrases that have not yet become part of everyday language should either be eliminated or explained. If you think "au naturel" will not be immediately understood, say "raw," "naked," or "natural" instead. Showing off has no place in a speech if it gets in the way of clarity.

- Newly coined words, or words that you make up, should be treated like foreign words if they are not in popular usage. For example, a student of mine gave a speech on "street-tique-ing." Such an expression might mean something to those who are familiar with the practice, but the rest of us need an explanation or we won't know what we're listening to. As it turned out, "street-tique-ing" is going antiquing in the streets—picking up old, usable items that people have discarded or thrown away. This speaker was telling us that trash can be a treasure. Once you know the definition of a word like "street-tique-ing" you can appreciate what's being talked about.

- Don't mumble. Breathe deeply enough so you have air to float your words on, then open your mouth and speak loud and clear. If you suspect you're a mumbler, exaggerate your articulation. Open your mouth and let your tongue and teeth and jaws move over each word.

- Before you begin to speak at all, take a few deep breaths. Exhale slowly to rid yourself of tension. This will keep your voice from quavering and give you the air you need to speak clearly.

- Practice breath control in your rehearsal. If you find you have a sentence so long that you are gasping before the end of it, shorten the sentence so that you can breathe normally. Take small breaths through your mouth as you speak so you never sound breathless.

DELIVERY DAY

The presence of your audience on the long-anticipated D day makes an enormous difference. If you are well prepared and well rehearsed, the audience will be an exciting

Rehearsal and Delivery • 107

challenge to you to skillfully share your knowledge with them, and to enjoy doing it. Your confidence and pleasure at being with them will be contagious, so let them show.

Remember that your performance begins the minute the audience sees you and realizes that you are the speaker. Your listeners begin to form impressions of you even as you're sitting on the stage waiting to be introduced, while you're being introduced, and when you rise from your chair and walk to the lectern. Before you say a word, your audience is already judging you by how you look, how you react, how you move. These are important moments for you, because they can affect audience reponse to what you have to say. You, of course, will be in control of these first crucial moments because you have done your body language exercises, and you know what to do. You also know to rely on Snyder's Law if anything untoward happens: "When the unexpected happens, don't agonize—improvise."

If you have not had the opportunity before D day to check out the place where you will be speaking, do so before you are due to speak. Arrive early. Check the microphone, the lectern, and whatever visual aid equipment you have requested. Know where you are going to sit as you are being introduced, and how far you will be from the audience.

Choose what you will wear with care. No matter what the occasion, don't wear anything that jangles; microphones exaggerate sound. Also, avoid any clothing that restricts your movements. Wear comfortable clothes, preferably whatever you wore for your dress rehearsal, so you do not have to think about anything but what you are going to say and how you are going to say it. A good rule of thumb in making your clothes choice for the speaking engagement is: "When in Rome, dress as the Romans do."

Women, of course, have more choices to make about clothes than men do. For most occasions, women would be well advised to look their tailored best. Fussy clothes are distracting, as are prints and stripes. Elegant understatement is the ideal.

> "You gain strength, courage, and confidence by every experience in which you stop to look fear in the face."
>
> —Eleanor Roosevelt

11

FEAR IS A FOUR-LETTER WORD FOR THE UNKNOWN

Anxiety is the bane of most speakers, and of nearly all novice speakers. So if anxiety is your problem, take comfort in knowing that you are not alone. In fact, in a survey most people ranked fear of public speaking ahead of fear of death! How this fear manifests itself and how to overcome it is the main concern of this chapter.

Being prepared is the speaker's best defense against fear. You now have a thorough knowledge of how to prepare a speech; how to know your audience; how to control your body language; and how to rehearse and deliver your speech. That knowledge alleviates the kind of fear that springs from facing the unknown. What nervousness remains should be considered a positive force that will stimulate you to speak with style. However, very often speakers do not recognize prespeech nervousness as a positive force. Rather, they interpret it as a flaw, or weakness, and by constantly thinking about being nervous they turn that positive force into negative anxiety.

Over the years my clients and students have shared their nervous symptoms with me. I've made a list of them, and if the thought of public speaking terrifies you, I'm sure some of these symptoms will look all too familiar to you. But take heart, for all my students overcame these anxious feelings in a surprisingly short time, and you will, too.

Nervous Symptoms

- nausea
- feeling faint
- terror
- dizziness
- loss of memory
- insomnia
- butterflies in stomach
- lump in throat
- dry throat
- dry mouth
- need to urinate
- pounding heart
- pulsating veins
- facial tics
- stammering
- stuttering
- flat voice
- hysterical pitch
- quavering voice
- nervous cough
- shortness of breath
- knocking knees
- trembling hands
- clammy palms
- sweaty brow
- sweaty armpits
- hot flashes
- nervous laugh
- quivering hip
- extreme fatigue
- choking voice
- tearfulness
- crying jags
- hives
- rashes
- blushing
- buckling knees
- suicidal feelings

All or most of these symptoms will subside or disappear altogether with experience *only* if your speech is carefully prepared, and if you consciously adopt a positive attitude about prespeech nervousness. You can learn how to handle this anxiety by converting your nervousness into positive energy. Here's how to do it.

First, realize that your audience is probably not aware of your nervousness. That may be hard for you to believe as you stand there shaking in your boots, but it's true—most of your physical difficulties are not noticeable to your audience, no matter how obvious they are to you. And you should not

110 • SPEAK FOR YOURSELF WITH CONFIDENCE

point the matter out to them! They did not come to hear about your jitters; they came to hear your wonderful speech. So don't apologize and don't explain. *Speak!*

If you are still not convinced that your audience will not notice your nervous symptoms, consider what would happen if they did notice. Would they all leave the room? Hardly. More than likely, they would empathize, observe that you are human, and admire you for your courage in speaking despite your nervousness.

There are ways to get rid of nervous manifestations that might be noticed by your audience. If you are aware of what the symptoms are, and of how you can alleviate them, you will be better able to control them.

Nervous Symptoms	Antidotes
Rocking back and forth, swaying from side to side, shifting weight from foot to foot, pacing up and down aimlessly.	Stand solidly on both feet. Root yourself like a sturdy tree, and don't move without reason.
Racing through your speech at a frantic pace to get it over with.	Mark your notes with ideal time cues so you will know if you are going too fast. Rehearse that way.
Touching your face, or fingering hair or beard, or covering your mouth.	Use hands only for meaningful gestures—that is, to tick off main points, to indicate visual aids, for emphasis.
Toying with pen, pointer, notes, lectern, microphone, visual aids, clothing, jewelry, glasses, or anything else.	Keep all materials at arm's length so you can't fiddle. Do your body language exercises so you are aware of what gestures to avoid.
Staring at ceiling, floor, or out the window to avoid eye contact.	Make a point of looking at a different section of your audience for every point you

Fear Is a Four-Letter Word for the Unknown • 111

	make. Draw a big eye on each page of your notes to remind you of eye contact.
Grimacing at your own mistakes or discomfort.	Remember Snyder's Law: "When the unexpected happens, don't agonize—improvise and keep your cool."
Using verbal crutches like hemming and hawing, *er-ing*, *um-ing*, *uh-ing*. Interjecting "ya-know," "and-um," and other air fillers.	Cultivate the dramatic *pause*. Practice as you rehearse. Ideas need air around them to give audience time to think. Silence is often golden.

> DON'T SAY
> "UHH"
> PAUSE
> instead!!

Understanding nervousness and all its manifestations will help you do something about it. By eliminating the outward signs, you can control the inner stress that brought them on. Psychologist William James pointed out that panic is increased by flight, and giving in to the symptoms of grief and anger increases the passions themselves. Therefore, speakers must understand that thinking about being nervous makes them more nervous. So Rule Number One is: *Stop thinking about being nervous.*

It will also help to examine your basic fears in a rational way instead of pushing the panic button and driving your body to react with all those nervous tics. Here are some common causes of speakers' fears, along with suggested "cures."

Fear: You are fearful because you haven't spoken in public before and you don't know what to expect. Or you have spoken a couple of times and did not think it went well.

Cure: Careful preparation and rehearsal will build your confidence before you speak. Get all the experience you can, and ask for feedback so you know what you did right and wrong.

Fear: You may fear audience reaction to your speech. Maybe they won't like it or you.

Cure: Focus on your audience's needs and expectations and you won't have to worry about their reaction—it will be positive because you will be positive.

Fear: You are apprehensive about your ability to deliver your speech—maybe you'll forget something important.

Cure: You will be in control if you are well prepared and well rehearsed in both the verbal and nonverbal parts of your speech.

Fear: You are afraid of failure.

Cure: Join the club—we are all afraid of failure. You must psych yourself up. Remind yourself that you have a valuable gift of knowledge to give your audience, and that they will love getting it. Imagine a standing ovation.

Fear: You're worried about your voice and your manner of speaking. Perhaps you won't be heard or understood.

Cure: If you have a naturally soft voice, be sure you have a microphone, and check it out so you know it's working on the day you are scheduled to speak. For clarity, be sure you review the diction section of Chapter 10.

Fear: You are concerned that what you are planning to wear will not be appropriate.

Cure: Dress conservatively and professionally. A dark suit is always in good taste.

Fear: You might be unnerved by your separation from the audience—you will be physically elevated above them, alone, up front, insecure.

Cure: This is a normal worry for all who are not professional actors or egocentrics. But remember that even the shiest of us has a bit of the ham in her nature and secretly wants the spotlight occasionally. Psych yourself to enjoy it. Concentrate on the rewards for your efforts rather than on the momentary difficulty of overcoming shyness. It's a challenge that will pay off in added confidence if you meet it head on. You may even get to enjoy it.

Fear: You have some nameless fear from a damaging experience in your childhood that continues to haunt you. It could have been some failure in performing tasks at home, in school, or in church that traumatized you.

Cure: If you suffer from such painful memories, you must do all you can to overcome them. Use the suggestions offered in this chapter for controlling anxiety. If that doesn't work, seek out a speech teacher, speech consultant, or therapist. As a speech teacher/consultant myself, I have worked with many people who were hampered by childhood handicaps—and all were successful in overcoming their problems, and went on to enjoy speaking. It can be done, with effort.

Now that you have dealt with all the negative aspects of nervousness, it is time to look at its positive side. The first thing to accept is that there *is* a positive side; I call it "positive nervousness."

Positive nervousness is the excitement you feel when you know what you're doing. It's a zesty, enthusiastic, lively feeling with a slight edge to it. Positive nervousness is the state you'll achieve by converting your anxiety into constructive energy. It's a mind-over-matter maneuver. It's properly channeling your energy to work for you, not against you. It's still nervousness, but it feels different. You're no longer victimized by it; instead, you're vitalized by it. You're in control of it.

Here's how to do it:

- When you feel the first unpleasant flutters or butterflies or sweats, admit it, welcome it, identify it. Tell yourself—

out loud—"There it is!" Go on talking to yourself. Tell yourself, "I feel it. I need it. I'll use it. I'll convert this negative feeling into a positive one by talking myself into it." Remember, nervousness is essential in public speaking. Positive nervousness is a speaker's energy source. It brings another dimension to your presentation—an electricity, a fire.

- Positive nervousness doesn't happen magically. You have to work at it. Talk to yourself. Don't magnify your symptoms; instead, lighten your burden and light up your performance with positive thinking. Psych yourself into it. Encourage yourself instead of wasting your time worrying.

- You can handle your nervousness by the attitude you take toward your audience. Rather than approaching them with dread, tell yourself you're going to enjoy them. Remember, enjoyment communicates itself—it comes through as warmth and affection. Audiences sense it and will send back waves of good feeling to you in their rapt attention, their smiles, nods of agreement, and applause. Plan to enjoy your audience. It will make you feel better.

- While you're at it, plan to enjoy yourself. A giver usually does enjoy the act of giving, so why not the speech giver?

- Here is a technique for handling nervousness used by many well-known speakers when they began their lecture tours, and for some it became a lifelong tool. They imagine the audience sitting out there naked! Imagining your audience naked tends to act as a leveling device—it makes you less fearful and injects some humor into your thought processes. It's worth a try.

- While you're sitting in a chair waiting for your host to finish introducing you, try using isometrics—minimal physical exertion exercise—to release tension buildup. All you have to do is squeeze out your anxiety into the arms of the chair you're sitting in. Let the chair suffer, while you rise to give your speech relieved and refreshed!

Fear Is a Four-Letter Word for the Unknown • 115

- In front of your audience you cannot indulge in overt physical exercise to relax yourself, but you can do it at home. Relaxation exercises, such as head rolls and droops, shoulder rotations and slouches, hands dangling at sides like rubber, trunk bends, knee wobbles—all of these movements feel good and rid the body of tension buildup. Stretching is good, too. If you exercise daily for general physical fitness, such exercises will also refresh you and release nervous tightness. Try the Royal Canadian exercises.

- At the lectern, or wherever you are speaking from, you can scrunch your toes in your shoes to get rid of excess nervous energy you don't need.

- Breathing exercises are among the best tools you have. Inhale deeply, then exhale fully to rid your body of stale air and stress. If you have a breathing exercise routine from your voice lessons, sports activity, or yoga, by all means adapt it for your public speaking needs. A good breathing regimen will rid the body of tension.

- *Act* confident. I mean *act* like an actor. If you act confident, your audience will see that confidence in your body language and hear it in the tone of your voice, and they will believe you are confident. You will then see from their body language (rapt attention) that they think you are terrific. That kind of feedback will be so convincing, you won't have to act anymore; you will be confident!

- Yawning is a good relaxer, though you should not do this in front of your audience. If you can self-induce yawning before you are due to speak, it will relax you and automatically moisten your mouth. This is a good technique if you tend to have a dry-mouth response to negative nervousness.

- Here's another simple, effective tool: Do not call your nervousness "nervousness." Call it "excitement." Every time your palpitations grab your attention and make you feel anxious, tell yourself you feel excited.

- Tell yourself your speech giving is like gift giving. Anticipate a happy response.

116 • SPEAK FOR YOURSELF WITH CONFIDENCE

- Remember, public speaking is like enlarged conversation. You're going to be talking to a lot of people as if you were speaking to each one of them in private conversation.
- Try creating a soothing picture in your mind to relax you. Escape to a stressless scene: a sun-dappled forest, a tropical beach, a garden of marigolds.
- Stare at something you find soothing, like a fish bowl, before you leave for your speaking engagement. Staring at fish in an aquarium is a definite relaxer.
- Get away from negative nervousness by delaying it. If you are unable to convert it to positive nervousness, try making an appointment with your anxiety. Delay it. Tell yourself, "I'll be nervous later, at seven-thirty, when it's more convenient." By scheduling it for a designated time, you can put it off.
- The single best insurance, and therefore the best way to handle nervousness, is to be thoroughly prepared and rehearsed. Once you are at that point you will have the assurance that comes to those who know what they're doing. It's a nice, comfortable, sure feeling.
- Finally, remember that ever-useful Snyder's Law: "When the unexpected happens, don't agonize—improvise and keep your cool."

Which of the techniques listed in this smorgasbord of stress relievers appeals to you? Take one. Try it. Use it. Remember, while you don't have to suffer, you do need nervousness. It's natural, and essential.

Unravel your old attitudes about nervousness. Get away from your old obsessions that gave negative nervousness all the credit. Go after positive nervousness by handling your tension in a new way, so that you can use its good effects to add an edge, a surge, a fire to your presentation.

12

INTRODUCING THE SPEAKER

Introducing the main speaker to the audience serves the same purpose as introducing one friend to another. You want them to know and like one another. The host who makes the introduction should excite the interest of the audience in the subject and in the speaker, and create a warm and friendly atmosphere. Though the host's introduction should be short, it is a very important function and should be carefully prepared.

In order to make a proper introduction, the host needs some facts to work with. If you are the main speaker, you should supply those facts in advance by making sure that the host has a copy of your biography several days before the speech date. How to prepare a biography will be detailed later on in this chapter, but first let's consider the art of introducing a speaker.

If you are asked to introduce a speaker, the first thing to understand is that there are very few people in this world "who need no introduction." For those few, it is sufficient just to announce their presence: "Ladies and gentlemen, Her Majesty the Queen, or His Holiness the Pope, or the President of the United States." All the rest of us need an introduction. Even famous people need an introduction that relates them to their subject and their audience.

For example, suppose you are a member of the local Rotary club, and you have been asked to introduce the actor Robert Redford as the main speaker at a luncheon. Mr. Redford may not need much of an introduction as a film star, but as an environmentalist he needs your best shot; you should give the audience enough to justify his presence as an authority on the environment, but not so much that you encroach on his speech. You should concentrate on his background, his concern for and work on environmental issues. Of course, you will be brief, but you must say enough to establish his credentials in this other role.

A good introduction must set the stage for the speaker, no matter who he or she is, by alerting the audience to the qualifications of the speaker that are relevant to the subject and to the audience. In a nutshell, here are your priorities:

- The speaker's name.
- The speaker's credentials to speak on the subject.
- The subject or title of the speaker's talk.
- The connection between the subject and the audience (if necessary or desirable).

If the speaker supplies you with a bio, you will already have the information to meet the first three requirements. How the subject will affect the audience is the reason you invited the speaker in the first place, and is the speaker's responsibility to develop. All that remains for you as the host or introducer is to prepare the introduction. Write it out, then outline it, so that you can say it over and over until you know its contents well enough to deliver it without notes or from a card. Eye contact is very important during the introduction, because you are warming up the audience for the speaker. Giving an introduction is really quite simple; it's short and good experience for you. There is a definite technique to professional introducing; here are a few "don'ts" to keep in mind:

Introducing the Speaker • 119

Don't guess at how to pronounce the speaker's name; ask the speaker.

Don't take too much time—the audience came to hear the speaker. One minute is ideal; two minutes is maximum.

Don't intrude on the speaker's subject—that is, don't tell them what the speaker is going to say about the subject. If you have heard the speech before, restrain yourself from talking about it. Just mention the title or subject or how it relates to the audience. Your job is to set the stage, not to share it.

Don't tell the audience what they already know about the speaker; reveal relevant facts they may not know.

Don't give a laundry list of the speaker's academic credentials. Mention only those that are pertinent or of special interest to your audience.

Don't read the speaker's bio to the audience—that's only for your reference. You must personalize the facts. Associate yourself and your audience with the speaker in a warm, friendly way. Even if you just met the speaker a minute before the speech, convey your delight at his presence and act like an old friend.

If the guest has agreed to answer questions after the speech, the host should tell the audience. This will alert them not to interrupt during the speech, but to make mental notes of their questions for the Question and Answer period.

One other thing for the host/introducer to keep in mind is that the minute or so before the guest is to speak can be an especially difficult one for him. The speaker will be listening to your introduction, trying to take a few deep breaths, and psyching up for the performance. Be aware of the speaker's stress by being careful of what you say. Don't embarrass him with excessive praise or gushing statements. Tell the truth. Don't go overboard.

It's a good idea to pay special attention to the manner of some of the many fine talk show hosts on radio and television, and the news people who regularly interview guests, before you are scheduled to introduce a guest speaker. They are masters of the art of introduction, and worth imitating. These professionals use their own rapport with the audience to prepare a warm reception for and create a lively interest in their guests, and that should be the goal of every host.

YOUR BIOGRAPHY: A VALUABLE RESOURCE

Every time you accept a speech invitation, the sponsor or host will request a copy of your biography. Have a basic bio ready; then you can add to it or tilt it to the needs of the particular audience to which you will speak.

The ideal bio should give your contact person necessary background information to use for publicity and for preparing an introduction. Here are a few tips on how to prepare your bio:

- Make it short. The maximum length is one page, double spaced. The ideal length is a half page, double spaced. Remember, you are not applying for a job; you don't need a résumé or any other long-winded epistle.

- Highlight your relevant credentials: accomplishments, important jobs, published works, associations, education. If you have an MBA from Harvard, we don't also need to know where you went to college unless it is relevant to your speech or your audience.

- Write your bio in the third person singular (he, she). This will help you overcome any tendency to be modest about your achievements.

- Write it in a businesslike style. Don't be cute, but don't be stiff either.

- Include only personal facts that are relevant to you as a speaker. If your subject is solar energy, it is not necessary for us to know that you are the father or mother of six children and also have two dogs and a cat. On the other hand, if you are speaking on the need for day care centers, it would be important to know that you have personal experience.

Here is my own basic biography, with an addendum tailored to a specific occasion.

Basic Bio

Elayne Snyder is a teacher, lecturer, and communications specialist. As head of her own company, ELAYNE SNYDER SPEECH CONSULTANTS, she designs and delivers communications seminars for corporations, professional associations, organizations, and government agencies, and holds private sessions for individual clients.

Ms. Snyder is Adjunct Assistant Professor of Communications at New York University. Her popular platform skills courses have helped hundreds of men and women develop their public speaking talents. Her unique Snyder Four-Card System has been featured in articles in *The New York Times* and in national magazines, as well as in her book, *Speak for Yourself—With Confidence*.

Communications is a lifelong interest. Ms. Snyder has a degree in speech and started her business career as a radio announcer.

Addendum

Elayne Snyder will address the Cosmopolitan Life Insurance Association on "Positive Nervousness, a New Way to Handle Speech Fright."

Speakers generally have little, if any, control over what the person who introduces them will say, but if you provide a basic biography, the host will at least get your name right, and will know which of your credentials you consider important. And if you complement your basic bio with a short addendum indicating the subject or title of your speech, you are reasonably certain that the introducer will at least have those facts right, too.

Unfortunately, many introducers will just read what you said right off the paper. That is better, of course, than having no introduction at all other than, "Here's Elayne Snyder," but it is far from ideal. If, for any reason, you are introduced with no real introduction and you feel it's necessary, do it yourself. I've had hosts review the details of my bio with me, check on the pronunciation of my name, show me their carefully rewritten version of my bio "in their own words," and then watched them get so flustered they've completely forgotten to do the introduction. If that happens to you, use Snyder's law—improvise. Without alluding to the host's failure, tell your audience what you want them to know about you. For example: "I'm delighted to be here to talk to you about expressing yourself. First, let me tell you a little about my background in communications. . . ."

If you have occasion to introduce a speaker, use the basic facts in the bio, but personalize them so everyone knows you have a warm and friendly feeling about the speaker. Here, for example, is an introduction based on my bio that does a good job of preparing the audience for the speaker:

"I think it's fair to say that most of us are nervous wrecks when we are called upon to speak before an audience. And yet, in our business we have to do it every day. Our speaker, Elayne Snyder, has good news. She's going to tell us how to handle our nervousness and make it work for us. She calls her technique 'Positive Nervousness.'

"Elayne Snyder heads her own speech consulting firm. She designs and delivers public speaking seminars for corporations, government agencies, and professional associations, and also holds private sessions for individual clients like you and me. Ms. Snyder has taught at several universities and has written a book on the subject called *Speak for Yourself—With Confidence*. Will you welcome please . . . Elayne Snyder."

Note that not all the facts in the basic bio are used—only those that the introducer finds necessary. The host is careful to involve his audience from the start, and to point up the need for the speaker's message. He then gives the speaker's relevant credentials, and restates her name at the end as he asks his colleagues to welcome her. This introduction is carefully constructed to make the audience want to hear the speaker, which is the main purpose of all introductions.

Your bio is also used as the basis of publicity releases or for the blurb about the speaker in the program notes. Again, a speaker always hopes that the publicity writer will do more than just print the bio verbatim, but even if that's all she does, you will know that the facts are straight and your name is spelled right.

Always take an extra copy of your bio along with you to your speaking engagement, in case the copy you sent in advance has been mislaid. Be sure that the person who introduces you has a copy. Your bio is important. Write yours now so that you won't have to concern yourself about it for future speaking engagements. You'll have enough on your mind then, concentrating on your speech!

13

THE QUESTION AND ANSWER PERIOD

The Question and Answer period is part of the speech format more often than not. When you are invited to give a speech, always ask if there will be a Q & A following your speech. Knowledge of the host's game plan will serve two important needs for you: 1) You'll know what to expect and 2) you can prepare for a Q & A. Both will help you to handle your nervousness.

How can you prepare for the Q & A? By staging a tryout. After you have written and rehearsed your speech privately, do a stand-up performance in front of an associate or someone who is (or can role-play) your typical audience. Naturally you will ask the person to give you overall feedback on the speech, but, most important, ask them to act as a devil's advocate for you in a mock after-speech Q & A session. The point of this run-through is to give you practice in fielding questions and in getting the feeling of how to conduct yourself. Have your colleague fire tough questions at you. Have her ask questions your speech suggests, probe areas where you speech is lacking, bring up questions your audience might ask after hearing your speech. Take the questions standing in front of your test audience, just as you will be standing in the real speech situation. Duplicate the real speech environment so your body language gets into the trial act as well.

This run-through will do several things for you. It will give you experience in handling the unexpected aspect of a Question and Answer period. It will give you the feel of handling yourself in the challenging arena of impromptu (off-the-top-of-your-head) response. It will prepare you to field questions, and preparation is a proven antidote to anxiety. What's more, a test Q & A might spotlight deficiencies in your speech. Listen carefully to the questions your colleague asks, because they might point to soft spots in your speech. They might expose areas that need more explanation, more repetition, areas that are not clear enough as they are. Then you can go back to your speech and make the necessary repairs. The run-through will also help you step back from the speech and gain an objectivity that you, as the speaker, do not have on your own. So use your trial Question and Answer practice session to your best advantage.

If your subject is complicated or controversial, and exact figures, dates, or other data may be asked for, prepare a tabbed notebook with your figures, dates, and other data in it, and then practice locating the exact material when questioned about it without fanfare, fright, or fidgets. Do it calmly, smoothly. You'll learn how in rehearsal.

Some other helpful information you should know in advance, such as how much time your host will set aside for your Question and Answer session. Ask. Then you can time it and pace it. You should also know in advance who will moderate the Q & A, subdue verbal fires that might erupt if your subject is controversial, and control the proceedings from beginning to end. If you are one of a panel of speakers, the host will probably want to be the control person—the moderator. If you are the sole speaker, you should run your own Q & A. You should make this clear in your early conversations with your host. In either case, you must have this information so that you can move smoothly and professionally from speech conclusion to the Q & A.

Now I'm going to take you through a hypothetical Question and Answer period chronologically to alert you to the possibilities, give you an overview of the situation as it typi-

126 • SPEAK FOR YOURSELF WITH CONFIDENCE

cally unfolds, and prepare you to handle any matter that arises out of the Q & A with foreknowledge, and thus confidence.

After you deliver the concluding remarks of your speech, which will sum up what you want your audience to know, to do, to remember, or to think about, the audience will applaud. You should modestly and graciously acknowledge their applause in keeping with your own personality. A smile of satisfaction would be appropriate. Do it your way. Check the time, because it's up to you to start the Q & A, pace it, control it, orchestrate it, and end it. Then, as the applause is dying, you should swing immediately and smoothly into your Q & A by announcing it to your audience: "Now, I would be happy to answer any questions you might have regarding the subject of my speech." (Use your own language, your own style.)

Be prepared to wait in case the first question does not come instantly. For some audiences, and because of some speech subjects, there is a real and seemingly endless period between the start-up of the Q & A and the first question, because the audience is changing gears from having been silent receptors to becoming verbal initiators. So give them a pause here. Do not panic in this silent space. If no questions come after what you feel is a reasonable wait—five seconds or so—do not panic. Act confident. Any discomfort you allow will be immediately communicated in your body language.

On the very rare occasion when no questions arise from your audience, follow these suggestions:

1. Have a colleague (or two) in the audience ready to ask you planted questions.

2. Or ask yourself a question (which you'll prepare beforehand). For example: "I'll start the ball rolling. Last week I spoke to an audience with interests very much like yours, and a woman in that audience asked me this question: [invent it, answer it]."

3. If after you ask yourself one or two questions, there are still none forthcoming from the audience, terminate

gracefully. You might say, "If you have no questions, I'll say good night."

If you come across an audience that doesn't ask questions, use Snyder's Law: Improvise your diplomatic handling of the matter, and you'll be fine.

Most audiences do ask questions, however, so you should expect to conduct a Question and Answer session at the end of your speech. If your host neglected to mention at the outset that you will answer questions, incorporate that important information in your opening remarks. For example, "Good evening, it's nice to be here. I'd like to thank you for providing time for a Question and Answer Period. Please feel free to jot down any questions you might have as I speak, and I'll be glad to answer them after my speech, during the Question and Answer period." Then begin your speech introduction.

Remember that pacing is key. Think of it constantly. You are the conductor. Orchestrate, give your Question and Answer period a beat, a movement, a music, an excitement. How? Take a question, then listen to it carefully, restate it briefly, and answer it as crisply, concretely, and concisely as you can. Practice will help you learn how. Always keep your audience's interests in mind. Tilt your answer directly to them. As you complete your answer, swing immediately toward the next questioner with enthusiasm and great interest. Repeat the process from beginning to end.

Your audience has already heard your speech, and they do not want another speech in response to their questions. They want a dialogue, a volley, an exchange; give them that in your expert, brisk, focused answers.

The Question and Answer period often has an adversative aspect. It can be you—the speaker—on one side, against them—the audience—on the other. The more controversial your subject, the more likely it is that this adversative tone will emerge and dominate the Question and Answer dialogue.

If this happens, your job is to be diplomatic, tactful, and sincere at all costs. Avoid being defensive. It's best to keep away from a confrontation that might develop into a heated "you" versus "them" contest. You can still have the excitement of a heated Q & A, but you must control the fire in it. Use Snyder's Law—don't agonize, improvise. Study how politicians handle such verbal brush fires with tact and confidence. Whether the exchange is hot or not, your job is to be honest, straightforward, and, even if it kills you, diplomatic.

The Question and Answer period can be a refreshing and lively experience for both speaker and audience. You're in control; try to make it memorable.

We've discussed how difficult the Question and Answer period can be if no one poses questions, but the situation can become awkward even in the face of audience interest. For instance, what would you do if suddenly twenty hands went up simultaneously when you asked for questions from the audience? The best way to handle this is to follow these steps:

1. Keep your cool.
2. Tell the audience you're delighted to see their interest in your subject.
3. Tell them you'll try to answer as many of their questions as possible in the time you have together.
4. Tell them how you plan to do that. For example, you could use any of the following methods:
    a. You might say, "I'll take one question from the front of the audience and one from a questioner in the rear of the hall."
    b. You could give individuals with their hands raised numbers and promise that you will take their questions in order.
    c. You could select questioners in the style of John F. Kennedy. He just pointed (a gesture I *don't* recommend), smiled and said, *"You!"*
    d. Having had cards handed out and an announcement made before your speech, you could draw from questions put on cards (à la Johnny Carson), and have a close colleague screen and select the best questions, hand them to you in an order that will get your Q & A off to a good start, and proceed from there. Credit the questioner whose name appears on the card, address him or her, read the question, and answer it.

e. You could select people randomly by identifying them by their clothing ("the woman in the red blouse" or "the man wearing the green tie") or by looking them right in the eye and using a beckoning gesture (do not point) to identify them.

When the questions come, they will sometimes surprise you, sometimes delight you, and sometimes baffle you. Suppose you get a question that legitimately relates to your subject—that perhaps you should know the answer to, but you do not know it? If this happens, the best thing to do is admit the truth. You could say, "That's a great question. I wish I knew the answer, but I honestly don't know. I'll check it out and get back to you. See me at the end of the program and I'll take your name and phone number." Then, do as you promised. If you don't know the answer, don't fake it. There might be someone in your audience who may know the answer, speak with authority, contradict you, and make you look like a fool. Then where are you? If you lose credibility, you lose your audience. There is nothing wrong with the answer "I don't know." Use it. Promise to get the answer and move on coolly to the next question without apology.

You must pace the movement between the questions and answers. Keep everything moving. Send out body language signals that say "cool," "in charge," "enthusiastic," "open," "sincere."

Suppose you get a question that turns out to be a speech from a long-winded, rambling bore? What can be done? Here are some suggestions:

1. Sometimes the person is known to the other members of the audience because he or she always does this "frustrated speaker" routine. If that's the case, you'll probably hear a choral moan. If you're fortunate enough to have a good, strong, sensitive host, the host might rush in and shut up the rambler by interrupting him and advising that a brief question is in order.
2. Or you could tactfully interrupt the rambler yourself with a hand gesture (resembling a police officer's for "Stop") and say, "Excuse me, but that's not what we're focusing on

here; I want to stay on the subject. Next question, please?" Such a display of authority will enhance the movement and the success of your Question and Answer period.

3. You could listen to the rambler's routine, respond with a pleasant "Thank you," and briskly move on to the next questioner without comment.
4. You could listen to the rambler's drivel, rephrase one part of the long drawn-out statement into a question you would like to address and answer it. For example: "The question I hear is, '_____?' "
5. You could take what you want from the rambler's speech (which sounds like you're going to get to the rambler's point, if there was one), and again do what you want to with it by shaping it into an introduction to your own question. Politicians do it all the time. For example, "I'm glad you asked that question. Have you looked at it this way . . ." Or, "That's an interesting point, but . . ." If the rambling deals with a well-known person and you don't want to talk about that person, you could begin your response by mentioning the person's field, constituency, or some other fleeting reference, and then get on to your chosen point.

Another type you might hear from during your Q & A is the person who lobs you a "loaded question"—a question based on a false assumption. There are at least 3 kinds of "loaded questions": One is an out-and-out lie; one is a question fraught with emotional or associative significance that hinders rational or unprejudiced response, and one is an honest belief in an untruth. An example of this last is a question that frequently surfaced during the national debate over the Equal Rights Amendment. Many audiences simply did not know the full text of the amendment. Therefore, their questions were loaded with false assumptions based on misinformation they had heard or read.

The speaker's job in responding to a loaded question is to confront the issue squarely, tactfully, and coolly, and to correct the false assumption with solid facts to give the best answer available at the moment. In a nutshell, you should agree, then disagree diplomatically. In the ERA example, you might respond to a loaded question like this: "What you are saying is that if the ERA is passed, we will have unisex toilets. I've heard that said many times myself, so it doesn't surprise me that you think that that is something the amendment will do. The fact of the matter is that this is a mistaken belief. Listen to the complete text of the amendment. . . ."

When a loaded question is asked, remember that the individual asking the question might be trying to antagonize you intentionally. You must give the best answer you can, keeping in mind the questioner's real intent. You can do that by correcting false notions, and, if it's appropriate, using humor.

The Question and Answer period has the excitement of the unexpected, but you can handle it. You may even surprise yourself with your concise answers to the questions, your-well-paced beat, your good sense, good humor, and your storehouse of information. Trust yourself.

There are, however, some don'ts to remember as you move through the Question and Answer period. Don't embarrass a questioner. No matter how stupid a question seems —even if the questioner deserves to be embarrassed, squelched, or ignored—be tactful. The members of your audience might overreact to the ill treatment of one of their own—especially if they are an organization or association or company audience with bonds among them that would create an unpleasant "you-against-them" environment. Even in a public audience where there is no group cohesion, a putdown might put an end to questions; people might fear being humiliated by your answers.

If you think a question is out of place, and has nothing to do with what your speech was about, you can respond by stroking the questioner in one of the following ways:

1. Say thoughtfully, "That's an interesting point," but move without hesitation on to the next question.
2. Link an idea you find hidden in the question with something it brings to your mind or that you want to comment on (but no one has asked you about).

3. Simply say, "I'm sorry I can't answer your question: it's outside of my field."

4. Say, "That's a very involved [or personal] question.... If you'd like to come up front afterward, I'd be happy to see you." Notice that this response promises absolutely nothing; you just sound like you would be willing to answer the question privately. If the person does come up at the end of the program to ask the question again, use your good judgment in responding.

5. Use a "redirected question" rather than an answer; ask a rhetorical question of your questioner. The question "Are you married?" is best answered by a swift "Are *you*?" Then move quickly to the next question.

6. You can also use the redirected-question technique in a more serious way. Ask a question such as, "How do you feel about that?" rather than give an answer. If you get an argument, use the broken record technique ("How do you feel about that?" again and again).

It is logical to expect questions to come out of ideas that you presented. In most instances you will be armed to shoot back swift, on-target answers. However, oral communication is fast and fleeting. Your listeners cannot reread what you have said in your speech, and they may not have been tuned in during every second of your presentation. The fact is, you might get questions that clearly indicate the listener misunderstood what you said. The best way to handle a question in which you are misquoted or misunderstood is to go back to your notes, which you know intimately from having rehearsed so often, and *read* from them. Find the point in question, and preface your response with a friendly "Here it is . . . you must have misunderstood. What I actually said was . . ." Reading is very convincing. If your notes are sketchy, approximate as best as you can what you said the first time.

If, in fact, you did say something that the whole audience agrees you said, but that you honestly 1) didn't know you said; 2) didn't mean to say; or 3) didn't mean to say that way, be open and aboveboard about admitting your mistake. "Did

I say that?" You might laugh at yourself with them. You will survive it all. Tell your audience what you did mean to say, and move on coolly and graciously.

If your Q & A is breezing along with plenty of hands waving, high enthusiasm, and a brisk back-and-forth repartee going on—good. Watch the clock. And watch your audience's level of interest. Pace the exchange. When the number of raised hands begins to dwindle or the clock runs out, tell your audience that you are going to take two or three more questions (be absolutely specific about the number). Then take the final questions and say good-bye.

You should try to leave your audience wanting more, not gorged. That people remember more when you tell them less applies to the Question and Answer session as well as the content of your speech presentation. When the Q & A is over, you could leave your audience with a short, appropriate closing remark. You could acknowledge their interest in the subject; comment on how much you've enjoyed being with them; tell them how much you enjoyed their bright questions; offer to meet afterward with anyone who was too shy to ask a question publicly; or tell them in one sentence what you hope they will remember from your speech (your speech statement should be part of this point).

And don't forget to maintain your positive body language just because your speaking job is almost over. Stand tall. Don't grimace in relief. Continue to project your authority and your confidence. Knowing your next move will help you to exit as coolly as you entered, so ask your host about it beforehand. Find out how he has planned to end the program. Should you sit down in the same chair from which you were introduced? Stand (on the stage or at the dais or up front) to greet well-wishers? Go out in the hall to receive fans? Leave the premises so that the group (your audience) can have their membership meeting? Find out, so that you can do it smoothly and with no discomfort. You'll be riding a wonderful high of satisfaction at this point; don't sabotage it by being ignorant of your parting move.

14
"SPEECH! SPEECH!"—IMPROMPTU SPEAKING

If you have ever said to yourself, "I wish I had said that" after someone else said what you were thinking, or if you ever kicked yourself after not opening your mouth when you should have, thinking, "I should have said this, this, and this," you're not alone. People who have no trouble saying the right thing at the right time don't understand what all the fuss is about, but if you're a member of the former group, help is on the way.

Speaking "off the top of your head," "on your feet," "off the cuff," or "winging it"—all describe impromptu speaking, the art of speaking without preparation.

Most impromptu speaking is initiated by a question: The boss asks you about the status of a job; a stranger at a social event asks you what you do for a living; a colleague pins you down for answers to a problem at a staff meeting; an interviewer asks you to tell her about yourself; a member of your family asks how your day went; a moderator at a forum asks for your opinion; a friend at a party in your honor points to you demanding, "Speech! Speech!" Impromptu challenges are ubiquitous.

You already have the makings of a good impromptu speaker. In fact, you do it all day long, every day of your life, without a second thought. It's only when you get backed into a corner with a question and the chance to shine that the specter of impromptu speaking seems menacing. But with practice, you can shine in any situation.

Successful impromptu speaking involves: 1) listening carefully to what's being asked of you, 2) responding confidently, with an air of authority, and 3) ending your answer before you get into trouble by rambling on and on. All three steps are important.

How many times have you heard someone say something brilliant in one short sentence, then kill it by going on for five minutes about nothing? Too often. If you say something brilliant, let it sink in, unencumbered by empty words. Less is better.

When you speak impromptu, without preparation or forethought, you're tapping your own resources—your life experiences, your work, your opinions, your ideas, your interests, your attitudes, your point of view, your fresh approach to the world around you. The trick is to take your material and give it like a gift to the somebody you're talking to. Don't be shy. Trust yourself and what you know.

If you're put on the spot with an impromptu question, if you are asked something that you just didn't expect, approach it the same way you would an easy question. Use that honest, practical little phrase "I don't know." Follow it with a positive remark, and never apologize. For example, if your boss asks you a question that you cannot answer, confidently tell him, "I don't know, but I'll find out and get back to you by such-and-such a time."

As in all forms of effective speaking, impromptu speaking requires you to blend your body language message with your verbal response. Make sure your posture says "I know what I'm talking about." If your facial expression is pained, even the most intelligent impromptu response will suffer. And don't forget the power of eye contact. Look them in the eye!

When someone poses an impromptu question, listen hard. Latch on to the subject and purpose. Always consider the source (your audience). What does this person really want? Remember, every listener you speak to is motivated by self-interest. Address that self-interest. Everybody wants to know "what's in it for me?" So tilt your impromptu remark to answer your audience's interests. Use the word "you" and you'll hit your target. "You" is a magic word that is translated to "me" in the listener's mind.

Give your audience the response asked for, make it short and to the point, and sing it out clearly. Mumbled brilliance isn't brilliant. People don't want to have to work to listen. Speak clearly so that you can be understood, and speak with enthusiasm for what you are saying. If you're enthusiastic, your audience will be, too.

Frequently, you know what impromptu questions will come up. For example, if you're going into a meeting at the office, you usually know what area you're going to be asked to report on. So think about it beforehand. Consider your audience (your colleagues at work in this instance). What do they want to know? What do they need to know? What could you tell them about your project that will help them? Ask yourself these questions and formulate your answers beforehand, in anticipation of their probes.

Most impromptu challenges in your day-to-day life are not speeches, as such. Most of your everyday challenges pop up in one-to-one encounters, in conversations, in interpersonal communication. You can, however, use the same tools you would use in putting a formal speech together. Focus on the subject and purpose of the question you're going to tackle. When you open your mouth, start at the beginning with an introduction, and, if you can think of anything appropriate, add a little spice to your remark with something specific like an example or a personal experience. Say something worthwhile, but don't say too much!

Here's an impromptu situation you will face all the days of your life. You can't escape it; no matter where you go somebody is bound to ask you, "What do you do?" The best response is short, informative, and to the point. For example, "I work for the YWCA. I organize conferences, workshops, and seminars for women." This direct no-frills response is fine. It answers the question and tells enough about the respondent to open doors for further conversation. Give the facts, fast.

The word "communication" comes from the Latin word

"Speech! Speech!"—Impromptu Speaking • 137

communis, which means common. Whenever you are communicating with someone, you are trying to share something you know that your audience asked to hear about or that you want to tell about. With impromptu speaking—whether it's the casual daily variety where you're asked about something simple or whether you're challenged in a "Speech! Speech!" impromptu situation—you're simply being asked to share what you know and how you feel about it.

In both the fully prepared extemporaneous speech and the off-the-cuff impromptu speech, you should focus your response as a camera focuses—on the main picture. The difference between these two speaking methods is like the difference between a portrait and a snapshot. In the prepared speech, your in-depth focus will result in a carefully considered, posed, lighted study—a speech that's a work of art like a studio portrait. In the off-the-cuff impromptu speech, your focus will be swift, candid, and instantaneous—more like a snapshot.

In both methods you use the basic speech building materials you've gathered throughout these pages:

Speech Statement—Subject and purpose

Speech Structure—Introduction-body-conclusion

Audience—Address yourself to their interests with your subject

Speech Specifics—Anecdotes, case histories, statistics, personal experience

You can prepare an impromptu speech whether you do it while sitting at your desk or while sitting at table at a formal dinner. Whether you do your thinking leisurely on a yellow pad or, like lightning, on a paper napkin, you can use the Snyder Four-Card System. And remember, impromptu or prepared, talk about your subject with your audience's interest at heart.

Because life seems to be filled with everyday impromptu opportunities, the following scenarios are offered to give you an idea of how you might handle similar situations. These examples are here for you to use as springboards for your own creations. And don't forget that you can give the matter thought ahead of time. Mark Twain said it took him three weeks to prepare a good impromptu speech!

SITUATION Suppose you are called upon to say a few words when you first join a new organization. How would you introduce yourself?

Example 1 "I'm Syd Beiner. I live in Sag Harbor. I also live in Manhattan. I teach English literature in New York City. I bought a summer house here in Sag Harbor because I found it to be such a charming, adorable, pleasant, and affable community. The people here tonight reaffirm that belief."

Example 2 "I'm Chris Filner. I have done some community work in my former neighborhood, and I'm very interested in becoming active in my new community. I work for the YWCA. In that capacity I work with community groups and I would like to share whatever expertise I have and plug into this exciting group."

Example 3 "I'm Mary Vasiliades. I've lived in this neighborhood for a short amount of time and I want to join with you to make it a good place to live. So I'm willing to invest some time and energy and work with you."

What would you, the reader, say "off the top of your head" in this situation? Try it. It's fun, and it's good training for you. After reading about each of these situations, even before you read the examples, wing it yourself. See how well you can do.

SITUATION What would you say in toasting a friend upon his or her promotion?

Example 1 "Here's to Irving. There is no one more deserving of this than you are! Congratulations!"

Example 2 "Congratulations. I know it's a well-deserved promotion. I think it's marvelous and I'm sure that there's more to come because you're moving along in such a rapid fashion. I'm so pleased that this has happened to you!"

Example 3 "I would like to acknowledge Barbara for her determination, for her hard work, for her contribution to

"Speech! Speech!"—Impromptu Speaking • 139

this company, and most of all for just being the very special person that she is."

SITUATION What would you say if you were at a party celebrating the birth of a new baby?

Example 1 "Congratulations to the new Kreiger. You're very lucky to have been born into this family. A long and happy and successful life!"

Example 2 "I wish happiness to this child and to her parents."

Example 3 "I'm so glad to be here with you to celebrate Suzie's birthday. I can see that she has great potential. I certainly hope that one day she will be in politics and perhaps even become president! Since she's coming from this family, I think that's a real possibility!"

SITUATION It's your birthday party and the guests are clamoring, "Speech! Speech!"

Example 1 "I'm happy that I made it through another year, and I'm pleased that I can blow out as many candles as I have. Thank you all for coming. It's really a delight to see you, and it's been a wonderful surprise."

Example 2 "I want to thank all of you for being here. When I built this house twenty years ago, it was to create a new and special life, and you've all been very much a part of making my life special and happy and fulfilled. Thank you."

Example 3 "I'm very happy to have all of you here, sharing my birthday with me today. I couldn't think of nicer people to have around. Thank you for being here "

SITUATION Suppose you were suddenly promoted to the position of boss; what would you say to your staff?

Example 1 "Good morning. You've heard the news. I'm happy to be here. As we get to know each other, let's try to keep our heads about us, work out any problems that come along, and accomplish what we're being paid to do. Between us, I'm sure we'll get my job done! Any questions?"

Example 2 "I am counting on your cooperation and you can expect the same from me. Changes may come, but we will try to do them gradually. There will be no immediate changes in personnel or anything like that. I look forward to working with you."

Example 3 "Good morning. I want to tell you that I've just been promoted, and I want to thank all of you, because without you it would have been impossible."

SITUATION At a friend's birthday party, everybody is asked to say a few words. What would you say?

Example 1 "Happy Birthday. Thirty is not the end of the world . . . here's to thirty more!"

Example 2 "To my favorite Scorpio, who gets much better as she gets older."

Example 3 "Happy Birthday, Jules. You've always been a headache, but you've never been a bore!"

SITUATION Suppose you were at your company's annual sales meeting closing luncheon and you heard yourself proclaimed the Number One sales achiever in the fourth quarter. What would you say?

Example 1 "I am extremely pleased to be presented with this award, particularly when I look around at my esteemed colleagues here today and realize the caliber of people I'm speaking to. Thank you."

Example 2 "Let me thank all of you for your support. I couldn't have done it without you."

Example 3 "I'm really thrilled and proud to be the person who has sold the most. I've always wanted to win this award, but it's like climbing a mountain. Now, at long last, I've gotten to the top of the mountain, and it's wonderful."

SITUATION What toast would you make to old friends at an intimate dinner party?

Example 1 "Here's to us. Long may we survive. We've already done pretty well, and I hope we continue to do so."

Example 2 "I'd like to toast Pat, who was a fun person in high school, who was a fun person in college, and who is an all-round loving, beautiful human being."

Example 3 "Here's to the wonderful old days and all the things we shared together."

"Speech! Speech!"—Impromptu Speaking • 141

SITUATION If you were being feted by family and friends on the occasion of earning your doctorate degree, how would you respond to the plea of "Speech! Speech!"

Example 1 "It's been a long haul. I'm glad it's all over. I plan to go to Bermuda for at least two weeks to recover. By then, I should be ready to come back and embark on my career."

Example 2 "I want to thank you for being here. And I want to thank the women's movement for giving me the understanding I needed to complete my dissertation. It would never have happened without you."

Example 3 "Thank you. I'm glad to have finished this enormous travail in my life. Perhaps I can begin to enjoy life now that I'm a doctor. Thank you for sharing this pleasure with me at the end of my struggles."

SITUATION What would you say if you won an Academy Award?

Example 1 "I would like to congratulate you all on your good taste. Thank you."

Example 2 "I'm just so shocked. I was shocked when they decided to make this movie. I was shocked when it became a commercial success, and I am shocked tonight because I cannot believe I won this award. Thank you."

Example 3 "I want to thank everyone who participated in this. And by participate I don't mean just the people who helped to make it, who acted in it, and who distributed it. I mean every person who went to the movie, saw the movie, and was willing to become part of it and enjoy it with us in the spirit in which it was meant. Thank you."

SITUATION What would you say to the assembled well-wishers at your own retirement party?

Example 1 "I want to thank you all for being here. And to tell you how much I'm going to miss all of you when I leave."

Example 2 "My retirement. I've looked forward to this for so long, and now it's finally here. I'm gong to enjoy it, but I'm also going to miss you all."

Example 3 "The YWCA has give me many years of pleasurable work. I have enjoyed the people I work with. I've enjoyed the programs I've presented. I've enjoyed all the myriad experiences that have been part of my job. I'll miss you all."

You can improve your impromptu speech technique by putting yourself into a hypothetical situation like the ones I described above. Use the Snyder System and practice your responses just to get the hang of it. Make a game out of it—it can be fun! Then, when someone startles you with an impromptu challenge, listen, latch onto the questioner's subject and purpose, and target your response to her or his expectations. With practice you'll be able to give a sparkling response that both you and your audience will enjoy.

15

A SPEECH IS A GIFT— SPEECH SAMPLES

Sit back and relax. You are about to be informed and convinced and moved to action and entertained and impressed with several speeches by some of my students and clients. The speeches are reproduced on the following pages, which creates a problem since a complete speech is more than just words on a page—it's living, fleeting, dynamic. I've emphasized that a speech should not be read; it should be delivered. With all this in mind, use your imagination as you read each speech, and try to envision how it worked on the ear of the listener, and how the speaker enhanced his or her words with body language when the speech was originally presented.

To do this, you might imagine what body language you would use if you were going to give the speech. What would be the appropriate posture, gestures, facial expression, and eye contact for each speech? In the actual situation, the sound and quality of the speaker's voice—the clear tones, the warm resonance, the projection, the carefully paced rate—had an effect on the audience. Consider that, too.

To get the most out of these examples, look at each speech from the point of view of the speaker, who worked to follow the Snyder System. Each speaker's primary concern was form and content packaged for his audience. Imagine sitting in each audience. Role-play a member of the audience in each speech and notice how it was slanted, localized, and tailored to fit you as a member of that audience.

Some of the speakers used cards, some an outline, some a full manuscript. Delivery systems, like so many aspects of public speaking, are a very individual choice. All of the speakers whose speeches you are about to read were thoroughly prepared and rehearsed, which liberated them to concentrate on how they delivered their speeches rather than on their notes. In each case, the delivery was a conversational and caring communication, reaching out to give the audience the feeling they were being spoken to, not at.

In each of the following speech samples, look at the speech invitation as well as the plotting components the speaker used to build the speech, so that you can see the Snyder System in action. This will help when you sit down to create your own presentations.

In the first sample, the speaker was invited to speak before one of my presentation skills classes. The audience, fellow students, were well-educated working men and women who lived in and around New York City. The invitation was actually a class assignment. Students were to give a three-minute speech on a subject they knew a great deal about that the audience would find new, useful, and/or interesting. Here's how the speaker plotted the speech after deciding on his single subject, dominant purpose, and pattern.

Card 1. Speech Statement
How to get a kite up.
Audience: New York City working men and women.
Pattern: Chronological.

Here's the speech:

"Good evening. 'When you fly a kite, it's like having a living thing in your hands that keeps you in touch with the infinite.' Let me give that to you again. 'When you fly a kite, it's like having a living thing in your hands that keeps you in touch with the infinite.' Only Willie Yolen could describe this experience in such lofty terms, not because he's a lyrical poet or a would-be philosopher but because he is reputed to hold the record for flying the greatest number of kites—178 to be exact—all from a single line, all at the same time. Can you picture it—178 kites from a single line, all at the same time?

"But the highs of kiting are in sharp contrast to the lows a novice often faces with an earthbound kite. So on this balmy spring evening with the March winds behind us and the weekend before us, I'd like to share with you some tips from me and from Willie Yolen on how to get a kite up and keep it there. And if you listen, I promise you'll be an expert at kiting as early as this Saturday afternoon—weather permitting, of course.

"Basically, all kites respond to the breeze in the same way, so the techniques I'll describe for getting your kite in the air will work whether you opt for the dime-store variety you remember from childhood or for the more sophisticated models such as the ones sold uptown at Go Fly a Kite, a kite store on Lexington Avenue. Just a word of advice on your kite purchase: Don't get such an elaborate one that you can't figure out how to put it together, much less keep it airborne. [Pause]

"Once you have your fully assembled kite, you're ready to fly. With your kite in hand, stand with your back to the wind and toss up the kite. Boost it higher by pumping rapidly in short takes on the flying line. Pump rapidly in short takes, flip the wrist—it's all in the wrists [demo]—release a bit of the string and let it get taut. Repeat this until your kite hits the desired altitude. It's vital that you remember to keep the line taut, so that it doesn't get tangled and you remain in control of your kite.

"But what if the March winds fail you on the beautiful Saturday afternoon you have picked for kiting? Don't despair, just enlist a copilot. Have your friend hold the kite vertically while you hold the flying line from approximately a hundred feet away. At the first breeze, signal your friend to toss the kite up into the air while you run like crazy against the breeze. Again, remember to boost your kite by slow, rhythmic pumping—use those wrists.

"Once your kite is up—perhaps over the Sheep Meadow in Central Park and away from changeable ground winds—it's likely to catch a steady air current and start to soar, as will your spirits, just as Willie Yolen expressed it. 'When you fly a kite, it's like having a living thing in your hands that keeps you in touch with the infinite.' But getting back to your kite, don't get too caught up in the moment and leave your kite to fend for itself. It won't. Watch out for sudden nose dives. If this happens, just start pumping again—use your wrists until you're in control. Be sure not to run if the line is too taut or you may snap it and free your kite as well as lose the rest of your afternoon.

"Another thing—be sure to watch where you're running while you're watching your kite. Don't kite in the street, stay away from power lines, and don't fly your kite with an approaching storm or you could rediscover electricity.

"In closing, I'd like to leave you with this one thought: Successful kiting is all in the wrists. So go out this weekend and experience the exhilaration that Willie Yolen alluded to, but try one kite before you tackle 178."

To illustrate how this speech was put together, here's the skeleton as it would appear using Cards 2, 3, and 4:

Card 2. Introduction
  Quote to tell audience what subject of speech is.
  Background: Yolen's credentials.
  Audience: promise results in getting kite up.
Card 3. Body
  Info about buying kite.
  How to get kite up—hypothetical example.
  Demo—wrist flip.
  Description, repeat quote.
Card 4. Conclusion
  Main point again—all in wrists.
  Humor.

The second example is that of a speaker who was invited to give a speech at an eastern college. One of the reasons I selected this speech is that it expertly adresses one audience with two distinct interests: women in corporations and women in their own small businesses. Notice how the speaker successfully bridged this two-pronged audience situation by giving both segments useful information.

Card 1. Speech Statement
  How business planning affects you.

Audience: Women in corporations and small business owners.
Pattern: Topical.

Here's the speech:

"Good morning. If I told you that I could show you how to make more money by just using your head, I'll bet you'd be more than mildly interested. That's what business planning does, and that's what I'm going to talk about this morning.

"Business planning is such a broad, amorphous topic that it's difficult to get your arms around it—so I'm going to focus on business planning and how it affects you, whether you're working for yourself or whether you're working for a large corporation.

"Planning is really nothing more than the pursuit of the best ends by the best means. Even in the best of times, planning just makes good sense. But in the current environment of 18 percent-plus inflation and skyrocketing interest rates, planning may well make the difference, particularly in small businesses, between survival and extinction. It's much like that old saying: 'Keep doing it better or you may not have a chance of doing it at all.'

"Whether you're working for yourself or for a large corporation, an effective business plan requires focused thought on several key issues. I'd like to talk about some of the major issues with you this morning.

"The first major consideration in business planning is to know your market. What business are you in, anyway? That sounds simple enough, but an enormous number of companies have not seen changes developing in the marketplace. They've ultimately paid the price. By not keeping in touch with the market they were serving, and knowing who their customers were, they suffered loss of profits and loss of market share. For example, when the tobacco companies realized that one of the fastest-growing segments in their market was women, this opened up a host of opportunities for products specifically aimed at women. As a result, there are ads geared directly to women—and Virginia Slims. Philip Morris, the company that created Virginia Slims, is a very savvy marketer. They know who their customers are; their customers are the eighteen- to thirty-four year-olds. Like most tobacco companies, Philip Morris has also diversified into areas outside of the tobacco business. It acquired Miller Brewing and 7-Up. Yet Philip Morris's diversification program has been much more successful than its competitors'. One of the major reasons for that is they've never forgotten who their customers are. It permeates their entire diversification strategy. Guess who Miller's major customers are? People between the ages of eighteen and thirty-four. And the same is true for 7-Up. That's knowing your market. On the other hand, there have been many companies who didn't know their market or their customers, and who didn't see changes coming. As a result, they just didn't survive.

"Elizabeth Arden, the cosmetic company, was almost in that boat. They lost touch with the fact that their market was really the eighteen- to thirty-four-year-old segment. Arden's former image could best be characterized by the remark made by one young woman, 'Oh, I know those products—my grandmother used to use them.' Can you think of a more devastating image for a cosmetic company to have? Not knowing their market hurt Elizabeth Arden's profits, and when Arden was acquired by a major drug company, they were in deep financial trouble. It took many years and a great deal of money to alter that old-fashioned image. Not knowing your market can be very costly.

"If you own your own business—whether it's a service business or a manufacturing concern—the same principles apply to you.

"Let's take the hypothetical example of a woman who owns a boutique in suburban Washington. In our hypothetical example, this woman's boutique specializes in unusual accessories and gifts. If the owner is doing her job right, she knows exactly who her customers are. Let's say here, for our own purposes, that they're mostly women in their early thirties with young children, who live in the neighborhood. Our boutique owner knows how to reach them. She knows what papers they read. She knows what they're willing to spend. She knows their life-styles and their tastes. She knows her customers, and she also knows who her competition is.

"Part of knowing your market is knowing who your competition is. Like most important things in life, it sounds simple and even obvious. Yet many companies—believe it or not—equate competitive analysis with taking their eye off the ball. One executive of a Fortune 500 company has said, 'If we just concentrate on doing our job and not on what the other fellow is doing, we'll be all right.' Needless to say, that company is not one of the more profitable Fortune 500 companies.

Taking a good hard look at your competition is not taking your eye off the ball. Not by a long shot. It's analyzing the people who are competing for the same market you are, and seeing if they've left a gap between the products they're offering and what their customers really want. Their gaps may be your opportunity for making more money.

"To go back to Philip Morris again, when they acquired Miller Brewing, the company analyzed the beer market and saw that no one had successfully introduced a low-calorie beer recently. And yet research showed the demand was clearly there for such a product. Phillip Morris saw that gap; they viewed it as an opportunity. Out of that research came Miller Lite.

"Let's look at competitive analysis from another standpoint. Miller's arch rival, Anheuser-Busch, didn't take Miller's entry into the market seriously. Too bad. Because in five years, between 1972 and 1977, Miller's sales increased almost five times, or 250 percent, while Anheuser's were up only 28 percent. See how competitive analysis can help you make money!

"Another way of looking at competitive analysis is by thinking of it as a football game. You can use this analogy if you are in your own business or if you work for a major corporation. The football field represents your major market. The opposing team is your competition. Obviously, if you want to gain ground, or market share, you need to analyze the opposing team, your competition, for possible areas of weakness that might be opportunities for you. It's the same in business.

"Competitive analysis—it's an incredibly important planning tool. Many times the competition is quite different than expected. Sometimes the competition doesn't even look like competition. For example, for years the sandwich was the typical American lunch. Remember when bread used to be called the staff of life? Bread manufacturers seemed to think it would always be that way. They didn't think it would ever change. And they never viewed yogurt as the competitive threat it has now become. Too bad. Yogurt did not replace bread overnight. Bread manufacturers would have had plenty of time to react. Competitive analysis could have shown them that yogurt was catching on as a lunchtime phenomenon. And it wasn't being spread on bread.

"So much for large corporations and competitive analysis.

"But what about our boutique owner? She has to know her competition too. Many small business owners are so busy carving out their own market niche that they think of themselves as not having any competition. That's not true. So let's look at what our boutique owner's competition is. Remember, she's selling unusual accessories and gifts. Her competition is the greeting card store down the block. Why? They sell gifts too. The department store two blocks away. And the bookstore across the street. Suppose the bookstore suddenly starts to sell records, too. Her market might be eroded. After all, records are very often purchased as gifts. What does our boutique owner do? She must react. She has to know what her competition is doing every bit as much as the major corporations do.

"So far, what I've been talking about is knowing your market. Knowing your market is an essential part of business planning whether you're working for yourself or for a major corporation.

"Now I'd like to move along to the next major area—knowing the critical factors for success in your market. Once you know what your market is, then you need to know the major factors that make for success in that market. If you took a look at the major companies in your business, or in any business, there would probably be qualities common to the most successful companies. Qualities like a high degree of asset turnover, high profit margins, low manufacturing costs, high levels of inventory turnover. These are the sorts of things you would look for if you were trying to isolate the critical factors for success.

"Many small businesses don't really know the critical factors for success in their operations. Many don't know which lines are profitable and which are not.

"A friend of mine has built a small business that imports fine linens from Europe. She sells them to specialty stores in this country. She has a very wide product line that includes embroidered towels, christening gowns, lace handkerchiefs, and things of that kind. She confessed to me that she really hadn't the foggiest idea which items she made more money on. She took care of business as it came along; she operated from day to day. Now if she were aware of the critical success factors in her business, she would be able to increase her business by simply de-emphasizing those items not producing a suitable profit and making more of an effort to concentrate on the more profitable ones.

"Another way of planning to emphasize the critical success factors is to ask yourself what your 'differential advantage' is. That's a long-winded way of asking yourself, 'What is it that causes customers to buy my product or service rather than my competitors'?'

" 'The differential advantage' is a term I'm very fond of, and I'll tell you why. I have found many corporate heads who could not tell me what the differential advantage of their business is. They stammer, 'Well—it's . . . better"; they just couldn't answer the question.

"If you want to make more money by using your head, you've got to know your differential advantage. You've got to know: Is the product demonstratively better? How? Is it cheaper than the competition? Will it last longer? You've got to know if it's marketed more effectively. The key thing is, if you know your differential advantage, you know your business.

"Does our boutique owner know why people come to her shop rather than to the bookstore across the street? She should. She should know what makes her special. Can you answer this question about your business? Do you know what your differential advantage is? You should.

"What we've been talking about so far deals with having a thorough understanding of the market you are in at this point in time. Planning, of course, relates to the future. But you have to know where you are before you can realistically talk about where you want to be.

"Some companies are like Christopher Columbus. Columbus sailed west without being sure of where he was going. When he arrived, he didn't know where he was. And when he got back to Spain, he wasn't completely certain of where he had been. In much the same way, a company often moves ahead without having a strong sense of direction. Today that can prove costly. Today you have to plan for tomorrow—whether you are a corporation or a small business owner.

"Planning is an active function, not reactive. It's a conscious effort to gain a certain control over your destiny. To do that, you've got to wrestle with the issue of where you want to be —not just tomorrow, but in three to five years. You all know that old saying, 'If you don't know where you're going, any road will get you there.'

"If you're a small business owner—where do you want your business to be in three to five years? Asking this question forces you to think about your future. Someone once said, 'Most of us might live up to our ideals if we only knew what they were.' That's what planning does for you.

"A plan for any organization, whether it's your own business or a major corporation, can be compared to a rudder on a sailboat. Without a rudder, the sailboat will drift aimlessly. With a rudder and a firm hand on it, the boat will go in the direction in which it is set. It's the same thing with a business plan.

"In some ways, setting your goals is the easy part. The next step, getting there, is a little tougher. How are you going to get there? Planning doesn't just mean getting more volume or more growth. Growth is good, sure, but only if it is balanced growth. Many companies grew rapidly in the late sixties through acquisitions, only to find ten years later that this growth did not bring increased profitability with it. Colgate-Palmolive is one such company. They acquired Helena Rubenstein with the hope of improving its profitability. They couldn't. After much effort and even more money, they're now in the process of trying to divest themselves of the company. The point here is that being bigger does not necessarily mean being better.

"The whole object of planning is to reach the goals that you have set for your business. In order to do that, you need to set short-term objectives. Objectives are specific tasks, short term and measurable. Let me show you what I mean. Suppose one of our boutique owner's goals is to increase her sales by 20 percent this year. To get there she's going to have to set up short-term objectives such as increasing her advertising, and perhaps running special promotions on certain items, and then measuring the response each month to see how on target she is. It's very simple—objectives help you monitor your progress toward your goal. Setting goals and objectives and monitoring them insures that your planning will produce results, and after all, it's results that we're after. As Peter Drucker, the famous management expert, said, 'Nobody wants to hear about your labor pains. They only want to see the baby.'

"Planning becomes even more imperative in an uncertain

economic environment, where profits are even harder to come by. In this kind of an atmosphere you need to focus on operating in the most cost-effective manner—that is, making the most out of the resources at your disposal. For example, our boutique owner might be able to cut costs by substituting a somewhat less expensive line of products and making sure that her inventories were no greater than absolutely necessary.

"You might draw the analogy between coping with an inflationary environment in running a business and in running a household. With food prices escalating, a housewife on a fixed budget attempts to feed her family by looking for cheaper sources of supply. She shops at the A & P, as opposed to the more expensive market that she has always used. She tries to serve cheaper kinds of food without compromising nutrition—chicken instead of steak. And, finally, she may even make more things herself—bake her own bread. So it is with a business: Operating in the most cost-effective way means searching for cheaper sources of supply, utilizing cheaper substitutes without compromising quality, and keeping inventories as tight as is practical.

"Business planning just makes good sense. It also helps you make more money. If you know your market, if you know your competition, if you know your strengths and weaknesses, if you've established realistic objectives and goals, and if you continually monitor those objectives and goals, you should be well on your way to success."

Here's how the speech looks in the plotting stage:

Card 2. Introduction
   Focus on how business planning affects each group in audience. (Tell them the speech subject.)
Card 3. Body
   A. Major considerations
      1. Knowing your market (corporate and small business examples).
      2. Knowing your competition (corporate example, small business comparison, examples).
   B. Critical factors for success
      1. Elements of profitability—corporate example, small business anecdote.
      2. Differential advantage—know your business.

C. Plan for tomorrow
      1. Needs—analogy.
      2. Setting goals and getting there—example.
      3. Short-term objectives—description, quote, comparison.
   Card 4. Conclusion
      Business planning helps you make more money
      1. Know your market.
      2. Know your competition.
      3. Know your strengths and weaknesses.
      4. Set realistic goals and monitor them.

If you should ever have to raise funds for a cause in which you deeply believe, the following speech, our third sample, is a fine one to follow.

The speechmaker was invited to give a three-minute presentation to convince her colleagues in one of my classes. The audience was made up of men and women in their late twenties through sixties, well-educated, middle-class, middle-management-level people working in New York City, a likely audience she might face in another environment.

   Card 1. Speech Statement
      Convince to give seventy dollars to Grand Street Settlement House
      Audience: New Yorkers—working men and women (see above description of audience)
      Pattern: Topical

Here's the speech:

"Good evening, and welcome to the Lower East Side of Manhattan.

"Some of you may know the Lower East Side as the place to go for a good bargain. I've been working at Grand Street Settlement, in the heart of the Lower East Side, for over five years, and to my mind the best bargain on the Lower East Side will cost you seventy dollars. Your contribution of seventy dollars will send a child to Grand Street Settlement's day camp for seven weeks this summer. At ten dollars a week, you can't beat it!

"Grand Street Settlement is a nonprofit social service

A Speech is a Gift—Speech Samples • 155

agency that has helped neighborhood residents since 1916. People of all ages come to us for assistance, and we can help them only because you help us. Now more than ever we rely on private contributions to do our vital work in this community.

"The Lower East Side is definitely a 'high risk' area. It is crowded; 182,000 people live there. More than 35 percent of the young adults are unemployed. Juvenile delinquency and child abuse rank third highest in Manhattan, and reading scores second lowest. Proportionally speaking, with more young people living here than in any other area of the city, these are alarming statistics indeed.

"In this environment it's easy for a child to fail. At Grand Street Settlement, we want the poorest of these youngsters to have a chance. But we need your help.

"Your seventy-dollar contribution will mean that from Monday through Friday for seven weeks during the summer, a child will be involved in constructive activities and good clean fun. Special projects involve the children in working together. Last year a group of youngsters tried to hatch eggs in an incubator in order to see the whole birth process. Another group became experts in solar energy, another in gardening. These are rare opportunities for inner city kids.

"Your seventy-dollar contribution will mean that a child will get to see other neighborhoods, other worlds. For many it's their only chance to leave the block. Last summer fifty trips were taken. The children visited the Metropolitan Museum of Art, Big Apple Circus, Gateway National Park, and many more exciting places. Weekly outings to a country club in Westchester were made possible through the generosity of one of our contributors—the kids would talk about these excursions for the rest of the week!

"Your seventy-dollar contribution can make a world of difference to a child growing up in this Lower East Side neighborhood. Seven weeks spent at Grand Street Settlement's day camp will provide wonderful experiences and a lifetime of memories. It may even change the course of a child's life. Now how can you put a price on that?

"Seventy dollars—consider it an investment in a child's future."

This speech touched the audience. In a letter I later received from this speaker she wrote: "Last week I got a nice surprise. Claire E. of our class sent Grand Street seventy dollars for the day camp. What a thrill!" The presentation was successful in fulfilling the classroom assignment and actually accomplished its purpose, even in its test run.

For your own experience, try to diagram the last speech, Sample 3, using the Snyder Four-Card System. How do you think the speaker laid out her speech prior to putting it all together? What was on her Card 2, the introduction? Card 3, the body? Card 4, the conclusion? As an exercise for yourself, try it.

Not long ago I asked one of my students who worked for a religious youth group to speak before a hypothetical audience of senior citizens in a senior citizens' home run by an organization of the same religion as my student's. The student stood and spoke about being old. In spite of her pleasant delivery, the speech was not a success, not even in terms of the response of her role playing classmates. Why? It was not her subject, nor was it a subject fit for an older audience by this speaker. What older person wants to hear about being old? Furthermore, what does a young person (age twenty) know about being old? Nothing. What the speaker should have done in deciding what to talk about was to look at her own world and choose something from it that would be interesting, appealing, new, or useful to her assigned audience. For example, she might have considered how the audience could get involved with her youth group—working on a project, sharing religious ideas, helping the young people with their religious school homework, or any other specific cross-pollination of the speaker's world with the speaker's audience and their world.

As I've said from the start, a speech is a gift. The next speech, the fourth sample, says it briefly and eloquently.

Card 1. Speech Statement
  Convince to try "nothing habit"
  Audience: Well-educated working men and women
  Pattern: Topical

Here's the speech:

"Good evening. I want to acquaint you with a habit that fosters creativity. You might use it when you start to write your next speech. The good thing about it is that it's simple and requires no effort . . . except, of course, doing it! Naturally, you've got to do it.

"It has worked for me in designing pumps, and it has worked for many others, including Edison, Dali, and Einstein.

"In my field, which is marine and nuclear pump engineering, I receive a document now and then that provides proof that something new has been added. It also proves that the habit that fosters creativity, which I'm going to acquaint you with in a minute, works. [Shows audience documents] These documents give me good feelings, added zest. They encourage me to try again. [Shows audience visual aid—a patent] This was my first patent that covers a new idea that adds versatility to a self-priming pump. The first page contains my name, hometown, and patent number. Let me read you this statement. [He reads from patent proudly] How about that!

"No matter what your profession, new problems demand new answers. For that reason, I invite you to try this approach, this habit that fosters creativity. What is involved? Literally, nothing! I call it the "nothing habit." Let me give you some examples of how great thinkers have used it.

"Late each afternoon, Thomas Edison would go to his office, close the door, and sit down in a comfortable chair. He would place a ball bearing in each hand and allow his arms to hang down at his sides. He would then relax, clear his mind, and doze. When a bearing dropped, he would reach down, replace it in his hand, and resume his restful state. In this manner he stayed on the edge of sleep without succumbing for about half an hour. We all know many of his ideas. We use their end results every day.

"Salvador Dali would sit at the edge of his easel, place a pencil between his chin and the easel—relax and forget the cares of the day. When he forgot to the point that the pencil fell, he quickly retrieved the pencil and started sketching the impressions passing through his mind.

"Albert Einstein once demonstrated with biofeedback equipment that he was awake when his brain wave activity indicated sleep/coma. Many think that his superior ability to perceive relationships was enhanced by this unique physiological fact. It was in this tranquil state that the relationship $E = MC^2$ came to him.

"Am I suggesting that you go to sleep on the job to become creative? Not quite! I am suggesting that after becoming saturated with facts and alternatives, that you have enough confidence to literally walk away from the problem and all other problems on a regular basis for short periods, and see what might happen.

"Try it. Try the 'nothing habit.' It may work wonders for you!"

Why don't you try starting with the "nothing habit" on your way to the Snyder System of putting together your award-winning speech—it might work for you, too!

The speech sample credits are:

Sample 1. "How to Get a Kite Up" (anonymous)

Sample 2. "How Business Planning Affects You" (anonymous)

Sample 3. "Convince to Give Seventy Dollars to Grand Street Settlement House" by Alice Obida

Sample 4. "Convince to Try 'Nothing Habit' " by Robert F. Paashaus

16

RADIO AND TELEVISION

One day you may be asked to appear on television or radio to talk about your area of expertise. The invitation might come when you least expect it. You might be in a management position and called upon to make a statement on issues involving your organization. You might be told by your boss that on your next trip to Houston to talk to the sales force about a new product, you will also appear on a local radio show to talk about the new product to the consumer audience. You could find yourself on TV because you are an authority on an issue that suddenly becomes the focus of your community or the entire nation. You might get a telephone call one day and find the local radio station wants your opinion on something related to your job, your association, your church, or your synagogue, and they want to tape your response right then and there. You might be walking down the street, or driving in your car, when suddenly you witness a shattering news event and are subsequently invited to the local radio or television studio to give your firsthand account of the accident. You might write a book and have to travel all over the United States and beyond to promote it on radio and television.

You might get the call to appear on TV or radio in any of

these situations I have just mentioned, and you should be ready. And you will be ready once you realize what to expect and how to go about handling the situation. That's what this chapter is all about. All the tools you've learned in the preceding chapters about the Snyder System are equally applicable for radio and TV work. The components of the Four-Card System can be adapted simply to media use. For example, an interviewer's question gives you the single subject and the dominant purpose. Focus on it. Give your answer in specific, visual language whenever you can. Keep your audience in mind (who are your listeners or viewers at this time of day?). Use a pattern if it helps you to instantly organize your thoughts. And, of course, use Snyder's Law: Don't agonize; improvise.

Suppose the call came for you to appear for an interview on the evening news television program in your area. What would you do? I'm going to give you some commonsense tips to think about and some exercises to do. Decide which of the following pertains to your particular needs and your particular situation. Then use the tips to prepare yourself for a hypothetical first-rate interview, and give a mock performance. You can never get too much practice.

CHECKLIST FOR TELEVISION APPEARANCE

Television is a visual medium, so your first consideration is body language. Your nonverbal signals can sabotage everything brilliant you say if they are negative. Therefore:

- Dress conservatively, but smartly. Solid and pastel colors photograph to your benefit, but wear a color that looks good on you. A tailored suit always looks right. Avoid splashy prints. Watch television and see how different colors look on the screen, especially the shade you want to wear. Does it catch the eye? Is it easy to look at? Does it enhance the wearer? Does the color fuzz out? (Red often does.) Does it call more attention to the clothes than to the person? Avoid stark white next to your face (beige and light blue are better). Don't wear ostentatious, glittery jewelry (earrings, tie clasps, necklaces) that catch the studio lights and become visual distractions; they do both you and your viewer a disservice.
- Similarly, avoid noisy jewelry; leave the jangling bracelets at home.
- TV lights are hot, but studios are air-conditioned and usually very cool. Dress with this in mind, especially if you are easily affected by temperature extremes.
- If possible, watch the show you've been invited to appear on to observe how it's done, what people wear, the chair the interviewee sits in, and the variety of camera angles that are used (so you'll realize that your full face, profile, hands, shoulders, back of head, and upper body may appear on screen, and that you should be looking good at all times!).
- Rehearse at home in a chair similar to the one used on the show. If it swivels, teach yourself not to swivel. If it's a couch, practice sitting in it comfortably and authoritatively. *Don't* slouch on a couch; it conveys carelessness. Don't sit in a stiff, unbending posture either, because you'll look ill at ease. If you're sitting up and feeling comfortable, you're probably looking just fine. If the interviewee's chair has arms, get the feeling of holding them without tapping or picking at them, or holding on for dear life. If the chair has no arms, find a comfortable way to keep your hands in your lap while you talk.
- While you're testing yourself on posture sitting in a chair, rehearse talking without using your hands. Save your gestures for the podium. You should not use hand gestures

on television. They tend to overwhelm the small screen, and can seem threatening and negative to the viewer, even if you had no intention of sending such a nonverbal message. Have you ever seen a top newsperson use hands to make a point? The answer, of course, is no. It's all done with voice and facial expressions.

- Rehearse your posture so that you're sitting up tall, not hunched or low. Check yourself in a mirror. Find a comfortable position that will send out positive and friendly signals. Find a posture that will relax your muscles so no tension is visible in your face or evident in your voice. Most of the camera shots are from the waist up or chest up, so keep in mind that your upper body might be photographed at any time during the show, and be prepared for it.

- Your face is the focus of the camera's eye, so you should assume that the camera is always on you, because you will not be able to tell during the actual show. Even when someone else is speaking, the camera may film you listening to catch your reaction to what is being said. If you look bored, the audience will see it. Stay alert and aware.

- Smile appropriately—not constantly. Look interested. If you look interested, the feeling is communicated and makes your audience view the proceedings with interest. Your facial expression is obviously very important. It should convey confidence ("I know what I'm talking about") and enthusiasm ("I want to share this information with you"), plus whatever else the content of your interview dictates. For example, if you were running for political office and were discussing a serious problem in your area, your facial expression would probably communicate concern, seriousness and strength. Former President Jimmy Carter was not successful in this area of speaking. Frequently, his facial expressions did not fit what he was saying, and it confused his audiences.

- Eye contact in speaking to a live audience is very different from on-camera eye contact. When speaking to an unseen television audience, your eyes should be focused on the eyes of your interviewer and of the other guests. More discussion of eye contact will follow on page 169.

It's time to think about how to prepare and rehearse what you're going to talk about during your television appearance. Consider these points:

- Television audiences, like all audiences, want to know: "What's new?"; "What's in it for me?"; and "What can I use here?" These are the questions you should keep in mind when you form your responses to the interviewer's queries. Answers slanted to your audience will help your television host deliver a lively, successful interview, which is why your host invited you in the first place.
- Take a look at the mind-grabbers (Chapter 1) to remind yourself what people are interested in, and try to include some of them in your responses. Telling an audience how to get more out of life or how to get rich, for example, has a lot of listener appeal!
- You won't have time in a television interview to be long-winded, so teach yourself how to answer questions about your subject in twenty seconds. Make your responses short and focused. Make them as specific and concrete as you can. Use your words to paint pictures in your viewers' minds. Example: "My book is about 'shyness.' It tells you how to make friends, how to be assertive, how to have happy relationships. The title of the book is 'Overcoming Shyness.' It has answers for people who feel anxious in social situations. For instance, I analyze the style of a very popular conversationalist, and reveal how and what she says and does at the parties she goes to."
- Be ready for probing questions from your interviewer that demand concrete answers. Illustrative anecdotes make good answers to such questions.
- Know your facts. A good interviewer will ask for specifics that appeal to viewer self-interest. Be prepared.
- Know when to say, "I don't know." It's far better to answer

a question honestly, especially if it's not within your area of expertise. If you don't know the answer, say so.

- If you are acting as the spokesperson for your company, you should check with your firm's public relations department for guidelines in talking to the media. Most companies have a persona for the press—an open policy or a closed, secretive one. Find out what it is and stick with it.

- If you're promoting something (a service, a product, a game, a shop, a show, a book or whatever), make sure you mention the name of what you're promoting at *least* three times during your interview. Five times is better, and seven times almost guarantees your success. Seven is best, because repetition helps your audience remember what you've said. Prepare and rehearse how you will mention what you're promoting. Don't be self-conscious about saying it over and over again. Build your responses on slipping the mention in nonchalantly. An interview promoting a book, for instance, is useless if the book title is not communicated to the viewer. If possible, take a sample of what you're promoting to the studio so the interviewer can refer to it, and show it to the audience.

- Try to watch interview shows, especially the one you will appear on, and listen to the types of questions the host asks guests. Then challenge yourself with similar questions adapted to your subject. Tape-record or video-record your answers. Play them back. Would your responses make sense to the audience you will be trying to reach? Are your answers focused? Concrete? Interesting? Have your answers successfully conveyed your own purpose? You might ask a friend or colleague to critique your tape.

- Prepare a list of suggestions for your host that details key points or questions that will help him or her shine and make you look good. This is especially important if the host has not had the time to read your book, study your background, or research the history of your issue. Some hosts ask for the list; some don't, but it's nice to have one ready.

- There are two kinds of pre-interviews you might come across during your television experiences. One is the "warm-up" interview, and the other is the "Are you worth having on the show?" interview. If you are invited in for a pre-interview with the host, or the host's assistant, remember that they are journalists at heart and are always looking for a good story. (See the list of mind-grabbers in Chapter 1; media people use them too.) In the pre-interview, listen to the questions carefully and give the best answers you can by making them interesting, visual, descriptive, and concise. A good time limit for an answer on television is less than twenty seconds. And when you finally go on air, do not refer to your pre-interview responses. Everything you say on air should sound new, freshly coined, conversational; avoid saying, "Well, as I told you before . . ." If, during your pre-interview, you tell the host something "off the record," don't be surprised if it comes up during the on-air interview when there's a dull spot in your interview. But be visual in your language; and you should be able to avoid those tempting dull spots!

- When you arrive at the studio take a good hard look around in order to satisfy your curiosity before you are actually on camera. Take a look at the lights, the cameras, the cables, the technical crew, the set, and everything else so that once you face your interviewer's gaze your eyes can remain focused on hers and on those of the other guests during the entire broadcast.

- If you are put in the hands of makeup people, and you think you look terrible after they do their work on your face, talk it over. Tell them what you want redone. If you think you look terrible and do nothing to have it corrected, it could affect your on-camera performance for the worse.

- Don't forget you have a purpose in appearing on a television show—just as you do when you're giving a speech. Keep in mind the points you feel you must make to accomplish your purpose, and then work to get them covered. If you are an author, tell your viewers the name of your book and what's between the covers that they can't live without!

- Your body language before you open your mouth is very important when you're on television. When you are being

introduced, the camera will be on you, and the audience's first impressions will be made in that instant. Make sure your facial expression says what you want it to say about you.
- There are several different types of microphones used in television. Here are some of the ones you are likely to come across: The *lavaliere* is hung around your neck by a crew member. The *clip-on* is attached to your upper clothing by a crew member. The *table-top* is placed on a flat surface in front of you. A *boom microphone* is operated by a crew member who manipulates the mike on a rod over your head and out of camera range. In all cases involving a microphone, my best advice to you is *ignore it*. Don't touch it, don't fiddle with it, and don't look or think about it. Just as the camera will find you, so, too, will the microphone do justice to your message. All you have to do is concentrate on speaking clearly.
- Ignore the television camera, too. It will find you.
- When the host is introducing you to the television audience, do not overreact. The camera will catch you. Even though the host is speaking, it is likely that the camera will be focusing on you. So look at your host with interest. A thoughtful, enigmatic facial expression is appropriate when someone is saying nice (introductory) things about you. Wear a small, low-key, thoughtful smile. Keep your cool. Avoid big foolish grins or any facial traces of discomfort or embarrassment.
- When you smile during the program, smile naturally, but not too much or too often; both communicate nervousness, whether you are nervous or not.
- Remember that when you are first seen by the viewer, a first impression is being formulated. Make it a good one.
- Keep your hands away from your face. Avoid touching your mouth, nose, ears, eyes, cheeks, hair, mustache and beard, and anything else you might find to fidget with. Keep your hands in your lap, or on the arms of the chair. Your facial expression, voice qualities, and what you say should convey the meaning you want to communicate on television to your audience.

- Avoid jerky movements of all kinds—a fast swivel in the chair, a rapid turn of the head to look at another speaker; a sneak look at the television monitor. Use smooth, easy movements.
- When the interview begins, listen. Listen very carefully to the question. Latch on to the subject and purpose the interviewer wants you to get at. Then respond in the best way you can, always keeping the audience out there in your mind. Try to satisfy their curiosity about you and what you do. Remember that the television audience is diverse. They don't all know your subject like you do. Localize to their interests; don't patronize. Even though you will be looking into the eyes of your interviewer, it is the audience at home you are really aiming to reach.
- Be positive and sincere. Be yourself; be natural. Enthusiasm is contagious, so be enthusiastic about your subject, whatever it is. Enjoy yourself. That, too, communicates itself.
- Use an everyday conversational tone of voice, just as you would in your own living room.
- Speak at a rate that feels comfortable, not rushed. Rushed says nervous, so if you tend to be a fast talker, slow down. A steady, unrushed rate of speaking makes you sound knowledgeable and self-assured.
- If you use speech crutches, such as "uh," "um," "er," "you know," "like," "okay," "so," or "you understand," in your day-to-day conversation, ask a friend or colleague to point out which ones you use, and then monitor yourself to get rid of them before you go on television. Try to pause instead of using a speech crutch.
- Try not to start all your responses with the word "well." Skip the "well" and get to the meat of the sentence directly.
- Trust yourself to give a good performance. If you know your facts, you have nothing to worry about. Be honest; the camera reveals self-doubt. If you don't know an answer, you can always say so, or you can use some of the techniques suggested in Chapter 13 on the Question and Answer period.

- Try not to be passive in your answers; the active voice is always more effective. For example, the passive form, "It appears that would be good," is much less effective than the active form, "I encourage that way of doing it."
- If you answer the host's question with a simple yes or no, immediately follow your one-word response with a specific example to interest the audience and elaborate on the point you want to make. For example, you might say, "Yes, and the couple I spoke to in Chicago who survived the plane crash told me . . ." (and then tell the story that adds evidence and interest to your "yes" response).
- Say what you have to say in answering the questions, but do it briefly and clearly. Aim for a fifteen- to twenty-five-second response. Rambling is forbidden on television, as it is in any communication situation. The interview should be like a well-paced tennis match—back and forth, sizzling with good verbal shots.
- Preparing in advance will help you to do a better job. Work on your first answer, and infuse it with a lot of spontaneity, enthusiasm, and eye contact (SEE). Try to say something upbeat and provocative that will interest the audience and will set the host up for further questions.
- Be sure to get your main points made early in the interview. Identify your purpose in doing the interview, and make it the main point of all that you say on camera. A two-minute interview may seem like an eternity, but it's over in a flash, so make your main point early and often.
- Again, keep the viewers' self-interests in mind, and address them thoughtfully.
- Be yourself. Talk as if you were talking to one person, even though your audience is made up of many. Television is a very intimate medium, and the one-to-one approach works best with it. So say what you have to say simply, convincingly.
- Keep your cool. Don't get mad at the host, no matter what happens. Some hosts have a battering style and will try to pin you down, accuse you unfairly, or go after you in some way, depending on the story they are after. If you ever

find yourself in that situation, concentrate on Snyder's Law: Don't agonize, improvise. And most of all, keep your cool. If you lose control or overreact, you will lose your credibility with the viewers. If the host is harsh on you, the viewers will probably side with you if you give them reason to be sympathetic, but getting angry is not the way to do it. Reason, logic, and a cool response will serve your case far better. Defend your points with facts, not emotions.

- If you are told to speak directly into the camera, keep in mind that only one viewer at a time is on the other side of that camera. Talk to that one person. The late Dave Garroway (the original *Today Show* host) said, "I talk right to the camera as if it were the one other single person who is here with me." You should do the same thing.

- If you ever find yourself planning to respond to a station editorial or doing a public service announcement, you will be facing the camera directly, eyes to lens. When you speak, establish eye contact with the camera lens as if you were in private conversation with the one person the lens symbolizes. At the conclusion of your remarks in this direct camera situation, do not look away, grimace with relief, look to your spouse for validation, or start to get up to leave. Wait. Hold your concluding facial expression until you are told that the spot is complete. Beware of "eye chop"—shifty eyes at the end of your remarks. When the camera's red light goes off, you're free to look elsewhere, but not until then.

- Here's a sample of the kind of questions an interviewee can face. In this example, the guest was there to promote her book. (Naturally, the questions vary, depending on all the conditions at hand: interviewer, interviewee, subject, audience, type of show, time of day, and so on.)

1. "How did you come to write *Thrilling Recipes of the Azores*?"
2. "How do you know so much about the subject?"
3. "What qualifies it as 'Thrilling'?"
4. Host picks one recipe and asks, "What's the story behind this recipe?"

170 • SPEAK FOR YOURSELF WITH CONFIDENCE

5. "What is a [asks about some odd thing mentioned in the book]?"
6. "What's the most bizarre 'thrilling recipe' in your book?"
7. "Why that one above all others?"
8. "Is it true you're working on a TV adaptation of this book?"
9. "What's the one thing you'd want our viewers to know about your book?"

The interviewer tries to use questions that will bring out the story and answer the questions that he thinks are in the viewers' minds. Here's a list of questions an interviewer used to explore problems of an adolescent alcoholic:

1. What was your problem?
2. What do you mean by "blackouts"?
3. Did anyone at school notice you were drinking?
4. How about your family, didn't they notice?
5. What do you mean, you had to be a con artist, a liar?
6. How much drinking are we talking about?
7. Didn't you ever think about what you were doing to your life?
8. What ended this nightmare?
9. How long has it been since you've had a drink?

Notice that all of the questions require detailed and interesting responses. That's the knack a good interviewer uses to make his program satisfying to his listeners.

Suppose you are asked to host a television interview show in your area. How would you proceed to put the interview together?

Here are some tips to help you:

- Research the guest so that you know a great deal about him or her. Make notes on special interest items that your audience might want to know more about.
- Prepare questions in advance.

- Prepare questions that cater to the desires and expectations of your audience. Ask yourself what you would want to know about from this guest if you were watching the show at home.
- Listen hard during the interview so you can pick up on the guest's responses (just as your audience will), and then ask the right questions that come naturally to mind. The key is listening to really hear, to understand, and to remember, so that you can volley on-target questions back to your guest.
- Don't interrupt the guest in mid-response. Hear him out. Otherwise, your audience will be frustrated.
- If necessary, clarify the guest's answer. You can accomplish this by saying, "Do I understand you correctly . . . ?" or "Here's what I think you're saying . . . is that right?"
- Let your viewers know what you as the interviewer are thinking. They may be thinking the same thing!
- Whatever you do, don't dominate the interview with wordy or pointless questions. Give your guest free rein. You can help your guest to shine by asking provocative questions and listening with interest to the answers.
- If appropriate, ask the guest's advice. Consider what your audience wants. Ask for explanations, evidence, demonstrations, definitions—anything you think your audience might be wondering about.
- Pace your interview. Ask your question, get the answer, probe for more if necessary, and then ask another question. Keep it moving.
- If appropriate, end by recapping the guest's responses, feelings, and insights in a short summary statement. Thank the guest and say good-bye.

CHECKLIST FOR RADIO APPEARANCE

Since the success of a radio speech depends exclusively on the sound of your voice and what you say, your only body language concerns are those that will be reflected in your voice.

- Good posture and a relaxed body will aid your vocal quality. It will also give you a feeling of well-being. When you slump, you feel slumpy; when you sit up tall, you feel tall.
- Your success in a radio interview depends on the host's ability to get an exciting, interesting exchange going. You can help by responding with enthusiasm and good visual answers. Try to paint pictures in people's minds with your words. Help your listeners to see what you are talking about by using graphic, detailed descriptions.
- Before the broadcast, the host or interviewer or an assistant will try to put you at ease, but once you're on the air, the questioner's objective changes from laying down the red carpet to putting you on the spot to get a good repartee going. Do your part. It's to your benefit to make the show worth listening to. It's so easy for a listener to switch the dial, so help your host.
- Before air time, the station engineer will take a voice level on you. That is, you'll be asked to talk into the microphone

Radio and Television • 173

in your normal everyday voice so that a sound check can be done before your broadcast or taping session. Be prepared to say something intelligent. They've heard "Four score and seven years ago" and "A-B-C." Talk about your subject as though the show were actually underway, and then when the show starts, when the red light indicates "on the air," you'll have had a mini-rehearsal, and you'll know exactly what to do. Speak confidently, in a clear, positive voice.

- Usually you are told how far from the mike you should be. There are all kinds of microphones, and they all require different stances. Take the engineer's advice, and don't be surprised if you are told to have your mouth much closer to the radio mike than you would when using a gooseneck mike at a lectern.

- Speak as you normally do when you're talking to one other person. Speak just as you would if you were having an animated conversation—at that rate, that volume, and in an easy, relaxed, yet slightly excited tone that will lend character to what you say.

- You can and should prepare for a radio appearance, just as you would for television. In the case of radio, you can bring a list of points you want to cover. Either put them on a large file card, which will minimize annoying rustling sounds, or in a three-ring binder, typed on bond paper that is safely tucked within celluloid binder pages. Refer to your crib card or loose-leaf binder only when you want to make your answers more concrete, more visual; do *not* read your notes. If the broadcast is half an hour, you could easily refer to your notes during commercial breaks.

- The audience cannot see you on radio, so make sure your voice is clear and musical, your remarks vivid yet simple, and your points selective and memorable. Repeat the subject of your discourse by name rather than using pronouns (it, this, that) to reinforce your subject in the listener's mind as well as to fill them in on what they missed if they just tuned in.

- It's always a good idea to monitor the radio program if you can before your appearance on it, to listen and learn what goes on. What audience is it beamed to? How long does the interview last? Find out all you can in advance. Fewer surprises mean less of the unexpected to cope with, which will leave you free to concentrate on giving the best interview possible.

17

MEETINGS

It has been said that the average American executive will spend eight thousand hours in meetings during a working lifetime. Outside the business arena, there are other meetings held and more time devoured by community groups, professional organizations, religious groups, and others, all of which add to the meeting-time glut. This chapter is dedicated to those unsung heroes who know how to stage a successful business meeting.

Since there are more meeting participants than meeting leaders, let's turn first to how you as a participant can contribute to an effective meeting. Your rewards will come in the shape of self-satisfaction, colleague appreciation, and meeting results.

The most deadly sin committed in meetings is talking too much. Tip: Get to the point. Monitor yourself and what you say; it will endear you to your fellow meeting participants.

No one, especially not the timid, the reluctant-to-speak-up meeting-goer, should go into a meeting without thinking about it beforehand. You can prepare something intelligent, just as you would for the impromptu speaking situation. (Remember that Mark Twain claimed it took him two weeks to prepare his impromptu speech.) Since you'll know the subject and purpose of a meeting before it begins, think about it beforehand, and then you can speak up with a well-thought-out contribution early in the meeting. Once you've made this contribution, you can relax. You won't have to sit there worrying about having to say something or worrying about what you should say. The fact is, once you have jumped into the fray and gotten your feet wet, you will feel freer and stronger about doing it again. An early contribution to the meeting will loosen you up to listen more attentively, and so will pave the way for greater involvement on your part. The longer you delay opening your mouth, the harder it becomes to speak up.

On the other hand, don't blurt out any old thing just to say something early in the meeting. Say something you've thought and feel strongly about. Trust what your good judgment tells you is worthwhile. Avoid shooting from the hip. You are invited to a meeting because the person who called it believes you should be involved, that you need the information shared, and that you have information to give. So give.

When you go into a meeting, remember your body language. It's part of your total message, even in a meeting. Use it just as you would in any speaking situation. Walk into the meeting room exuding positive nonverbal signals. How? Walk tall. Smile. Look people in the eye. Don't fidget. Develop an air of confidence, an authoritative presence, and back it up by being prepared.

While you're in the meeting, sit back and relax. Have you ever seen the boss or the client sitting on the edge of a chair? It's a powerless pose. Sit where you can be seen and heard. Remember, too, that what you wear will influence what you say; dress for a business meeting like a business person.

When you speak, speak with authority. Say what you mean and mean what you say. If you sound unsure, your contribution will not be taken seriously by anyone. Speak for yourself—with confidence.

If you are interrupted by anyone other than the boss, keep talking, and direct your remarks to the boss or the meeting leader. Ignore the interrupter. Do not acknowledge him with eye contact or you'll lose the floor.

Meetings • 177

Now that you know the protocol for a meeting participant, let's look at some tips you can use when you're the meeting leader. From the start of the meeting, project your authority, your confidence, your know-how. If you let your people know they are in good hands, you'll retain control of the meeting. If you seem unsure, sound hesitant or weak, the meeting leadership will be taken over by the strongest—or the loudest—of the participants.

Orchestrate and pace your meeting with a prepared agenda (like a good speech script) that aims to focus attention, to heighten interest on areas of mutual concern, and to get the meeting purpose accomplished.

Make sure that your delivery ignites participant interest, and try to call on people who will add even more energy to your meeting—the "upbeat" types, the doers, the thinkers, the givers (whether or not they raise their hands).

Avoid lulls, gaps, and cross-conversations by asking for directional input from others in the meeting. A good way to do this is to say, "OK, now where do we go?" Or, "Where are we now?" Or, "What's the next logical action?"

Be diplomatic. Be considerate. A meeting leader gets more out of participants who feel well treated and respected. Even more comes to the leader who uses validation, as for example with such a remark as, "That was a great suggestion, Mary!"

As the meeting moves along, monitor your talkers to keep participants on the subject at hand. Gently interrupt if they stray. Keep reminding your attendees of the subject before them, and what you want from them, so that everyone is on the same wave length. People do get tired and distracted, so do your best to help them follow you. When someone strays on to a new idea, express appreciation for their contribution and promise to return to their idea after you finish with the subject being discussed.

And make sure that you listen. Careful listening will help you control the proceedings better and keep the meeting moving on course, and will make your participants feel valued. Your attentive listening will also set an example for the rest of the group, although you should not hesitate to ask for the participants' attention, if necessary.

There are ways of handling common meeting types; these

tips may help. After your "Know-it-all" speaks, ask the others to comment on what he said. Bring out the "Silent One" by asking her a question you know she knows the answer to, and will feel reasonably confident answering. Then praise her. Ask the "Debater" for hard facts to back up his generalizations. After "Irrelevant" makes his irrelevant remark, stroke him by saying, "That's an interesting point," and turn the remark around to make it relevant.

An enthusiastic, prepared meeting leader can handle any meeting situation, and you can, too.

The rest of this chapter will show you, in more detail, how to apply your speaker's tools to the world of meetings. First, what is a meeting? The answer is that a meeting is a group of people (two or more) talking together for a clearly defined purpose.

Why should you have a meeting? Because it's the fastest way of passing information to those who need it. Meetings save time wasted by sending and answering memos and letters—and time is money. Meetings give you instant feedback, reactions, ideas, opinions, and approaches that you can use to move ahead. Meetings, if handled knowledgeably, reduce tension and resolve differing points of view through open discussion. Meetings can use many minds to solve problems, reach decisions, and reduce the probability of doing the wrong thing. If you can accomplish one or more of these reasons for having a meeting, call a meeting. Otherwise, send a memo, pick up the phone, or make the decision by yourself.

Once you decide that a meeting is essential, you have to do the ground work to insure your meeting's success. You need a game plan, a way of approaching and accomplishing your meeting purpose. Many of the tips and tools you have already gathered from the speech-preparation requirements are applicable to meetings, too. Use them. If you are calling a meeting, you are the host, and, like any host, you've got to do everything from inviting the participants to running the show.

MEETING LEADER RESPONSIBILITIES

- Decide whom to invite. Remember, invite only those individuals who have either something to offer the meeting or something to get out of the meeting.
- Schedule the meeting. Set the date, time, and length of the meeting.
- Reserve the room for the meeting. Consider creature comforts, possible interruptions, and costs if you use an outside facility.
- Prepare a meeting plan (use the Snyder Four-Card System). Know your subject and purpose. In the introduction, set the tone for the meeting and tell what your meeting objective is. In the body of your meeting, work toward achieving your objective. In the conclusion, recap and assign follow-up tasks.
- An agenda can be written by you, the meeting leader; or it can be written after the meeting leader asks the prospective participants for their input prior to the meeting (by way of a written questionnaire or memo); or the agenda can be developed at the outset of the meeting by the participants in light of the thrust and objectives of the meeting. The group-made agenda can make running an efficient meeting much easier, since it is time-budgeted by the participants, who then share the responsibility of sticking to their own guidelines.
- If it's your meeting, be a good host. Provide a working environment: good ventilation, decent chairs, no smoking, place cards on the table if everyone doesn't know everyone else, tables and chairs arranged with the needs of the meeting as well as the comfort of the attendees in mind, a jug of water and cups, coffee and Danish if it's a morning meeting, pens, pencils, pads, chalk, chalkboard, eraser, flip charts, paper, film (racked and ready to go), slide projector (slides in order, rehearsed, and ready to go), overhead projector (planned and positioned with acetates in

order). These are just some of the many things that you, as host, as meeting caller, should think about and provide, as needed.

- If you and all attendees know each other, that's one less concern. If that isn't the case, it's your job to welcome and introduce everybody.
- A good meeting leader starts a meeting exactly on time, when scheduled, not ten minutes after that time. Start by sending a message that sets the tone of your meeting—expressing enthusiasm and confidence of accomplishment. Your attitude determines the participants' response.

Now, let's take a look at what's involved in running each type of meeting.

Staff Meeting

A traditional staff meeting requires that the meeting leader fulfill all of the responsibilities just discussed. As leader, you must *control* and *structure* the meeting; this doesn't happen by itself. You lead your group by projecting confidence, concern, and control. The participants will respond positively if you seem to know what you're doing. Your introductory statement will set the stage and should announce the meeting's objectives. Use body language to complement your verbal message. Just as you do in a speech, give your attendees necessary background information, stimulate their involvement in the meeting, and whet their appetites to get the job done by demonstrating your own enthusiasm for the project.

If you know *Robert's Rules of Order,* you know that the "motion" is the centerpiece of the process. It's a focusing tool, as is your speech statement. Use it. You don't have to use the language of parliamentary procedure, but you can accomplish the same thing by keeping your participants' attention focused on the topic at hand, and nipping offshoot discussions in the bud.

The motion procedure works like this: A motion is made

by one member, seconded by another member, then discussed until it is finally voted upon. You don't have to follow this formal procedure, but sticking loosely to a motion pattern will help you to accomplish your goals by keeping your participants' attention on one item at a time, discussing it thoroughly, and resolving it one way or the other before moving on to the next item.

At the end of your meeting, summarize, as you do when concluding a speech, what you have done and tell your people what's next. Make sure everyone knows what they have to do as follow-up by giving assignments, and keeping a record of who's to do what. Set your next meeting date for when the reports on assignments can be given or the implementation of this meeting's goals can be reported upon. And make sure to thank your people for their participation in the meeting and for their hard work in following up on the meeting ideas. People appreciate recognition—it's like applause.

Problem-Solving Meeting

The success of the problem-solving meeting depends on the ability of the leader not to lead, but to *share* the leadership with the participants. A group of up to twelve or fifteen participants is ideal for this meeting type. Everybody contributes and is responsible for reaching a decision. The leader serves the group, and helps the group, but does not lead the group in the traditional sense. What the leader does do is encourage productivity and try to keep things running smoothly by recognizing the feelings, emotions, and conflicts that can impede meeting progress. Problem solving is a shared experience in which trust builds as people work together.

The five steps involved in the problem-solving meeting overlap each other; one step is almost a part of the one before and of the one after. In this group-oriented process, the leader opens the meeting by introducing the agenda to be developed by the participants.

Once the agenda is listed, priorities set, and time budgeted, the leader focuses group attention on the first item by making a short introductory statement that gives whatever background information is necessary, just like any good speech introduction. Make sure that, as the leader, your introduction arouses a sense of dissatisfaction about the problem under discussion. Why? Because until a person's mind is disturbed, the thinking process is slow to get moving. In the opening statement, the problem should be stated and made to sound dire, looming, urgent, in need of action. Make the issue visual; you'll get results. If it doesn't sound like a pressing problem, it won't be treated like one. It's as simple as that.

In the second step the group addresses what caused the problem. As leader, you should encourage participants to share everything they know about the problem and its causes. Let them feel you value their contributions no matter how insignificant they might seem in light of a weightier remark made by another member of the group. Tell your people you want their opinions, their thoughts, their suppositions. It is important to see all aspects of the problem and what caused it. Probe with questions like: How did we get here? How long has this problem existed? What started the problem? What are the effects of the problem right now? What will the effects be in the future?

The third step of the problem-solving process is to list possible solutions. Ask someone to act as recorder and write down every suggestion so that nothing slips between the cracks. It is a good idea to list the solution suggestions on a chalkboard in front of your group as a thought provoker. And don't forget to introduce the brainstorm process to exhaust every solution possibility (see the section on creative meetings that follows).

Step four in the problem-solving meeting is to select the best solution. This is the very heart of the problem-solving process.

Since you are the leader, your ability to probe and listen is crucial to the success of this step. Your job is to help your participants examine the strengths and weaknesses of their list of possible solutions, to strike out those that hold no promise, and to carefully reconsider the strongest in order to come up with the very best solution (or solutions, if more than one is possible).

To accomplish this task, you should ask questions that will help your group to thoroughly analyze the better solutions from every angle. Focus on possible obstacles that might hinder the carrying out of a solution. Ask questions to find out if there are resources available to implement the chosen solution. Probe to determine if the solution is appropriate for your organization. Question whether the solution, once implemented, would make a significant difference. Is the solution the most cost-efficient? Will there be side effects? Question. Question. Listen. Listen. Work to find the best possible solution, the one everyone in the group believes in and can live with.

The final step in the problem-solving meeting is implementing the best solution. It is up to you, the leader, to follow through in putting the solution into action. Assign the necessary tasks to the members of the group. Put it all down on paper and issue a memo summarizing the results of the meeting, and reiterating the actions each individual is responsible for to implement the solution. And arrange for a follow-up meeting, scheduled within a reasonable period of time, to share the burden and examine the progress.

Creative Meeting

The heart of the creative meeting is that spontaneous creature, the brainstorm. But, as leader, you certainly shouldn't plunge into a creative meeting without performing the routine meeting preliminaries. Rather, you should plan and run a creative meeting with much of the forethought and structure of more formal meetings.

Once your group knows your intent to brainstorm, make sure that the participants understand the process if they don't already; tell them how you will run it, and, most important of all, tell them what you want them to focus on in the brainstorm session.

Brainstorming is a free-flowing, uninhibited stimulation of

ideas from a mentally active group of people who feel at ease and unthreatened. The objective is to come up with as many ideas as possible—good and not so good—to solve the problem or answer the question at hand. Again, it's helpful to have ideas numbered and listed clearly on a chalk board or flip chart that all participants can see.

The leader has a unique job in the creative meeting that involves body language more than spoken language. The leader of a creative session does virtually nothing—and that's very important. There are, of course, some introductory leadership chores to be performed to get the brainstorm going: The leader needs to tell the participants what the problem is before the brainstorm can begin. It is also imperative that the leader assure the group that there will be no criticism and no judgments made on their offerings. Every idea is welcome and should be voiced, regardless of how crazy it may seem. A good brainstorm is uninhibited, unedited, and free in every way so that minds will open and pour out whatever pops into them.

As already mentioned, you as leader must hold back; say almost nothing once the brainstorm is moving along. Instead, use body language to encourage offerings. Point to the problem displayed on the chalkboard; use an encouraging gesture with your hands to invite people's ideas; use the pause. Then wait patiently until ideas are voiced; talk stops the flow and interrupts concentration whereas silent pauses seem to act as a stimulant.

Training Meeting

Call a training meeting when you want to teach your people something new. You might call such meetings to demonstrate a new piece of equipment they will have to use, to teach them how to write memos clearly, how to speak a foreign language before going overseas, or how to use a videotape machine to train their own staff. In each instance, this type of meeting is a hands-on instructional experience.

As leader, you should spoon-feed your group the instruction in a clear, easy-to-understand format, using simple language and visual aids, if necessary. The chronological approach ("First you do this, then you do this . . . ") is usually most effective in training meetings. People learn more quickly if the leader creates a relaxed, nonthreatening, supportive atmosphere, one that permits them to learn at their own pace and to feel free to discuss the procedures among themselves.

Once you have presented the learning material, invite the participants to run the equipment (or practice the newly learned skill) themselves. Ask them questions to be sure they understand. Offer to answer any questions they might have. And remember to validate. People need a pat on the head!

A good meeting, like a good speech, depends on preparation, participant need and expectations, and putting together the vital components. A good meeting leader thinks about the meeting far in advance and performs all the preliminary/host duties as well as the presentation/leadership preparation. People spend so much of their lives in meetings that somebody like you could make the meeting experience far more satisfying for them—and accomplish your goals to boot.

Briefing

A briefing is a presentation of business or technical material delivered by an expert to a concerned audience. It is a speech given to a relatively small audience, usually from within your own organization, to people with whom you interact on an ongoing basis. In all other ways, however, a briefing is quite similar to a public speech or presentation, and can be approached and put together in much the same way.

Briefing topics are exclusively business-related, although the specific subject and focus will come out of your own area of business expertise. The briefing objective is either to inform, instruct, convince, or motivate. You want results in a briefing. And, as you are preparing for it, you should be asking yourself what you must tell your colleagues in order to achieve the results you are after. The skill to deliver an effective briefing is one more essential tool you can add to your communication repertoire.

18
FORMIDABLE FORMATS: WORKSHOPS, SEMINARS, PANELS

Workshops and seminars share the same purpose—they teach. The word "seminar" comes from the Latin root *semin*, "seed." A seminar is the seeding of information, the planting of knowledge. Like a workshop, a seminar disseminates information. Both are used to explain, to teach. The leader tells; the participants learn and do.

Ideally, a workshop or seminar should have no more than twenty to thirty participants. As leader, your first consideration in a workshop or seminar is the same as it is with a speech: the audience. Keep your audience in mind as you prepare tasks for the workshop that are suitable for individual or group application.

The workshop game plan, like the speech, has a structure. And the Snyder Four-Card System is just as helpful in planning a workshop as it is in planning a speech. You will begin your workshop with appropriate opening remarks (your introduction), telling the group what they're going to learn and do in the workshop. In the body of your workshop plan, you elaborate on the workshop theme, and in your conclusion you restate what you've told them and wrap up by telling them what you want them to do with the new information.

188 • SPEAK FOR YOURSELF WITH CONFIDENCE

After you've finished speaking, the hands-on learning begins.

The term "workshop" is often used as a synonym for meetings, conferences, seminars, and colloquiums of all kinds, some of them involving huge numbers of people. But the classic workshop is for a small group of people who get together to learn about a specific subject from an expert. The nomenclature indicates the form. It is a "work shop," not a meeting, lecture, or forum, though all have elements in common. The workshop is run by a leader, who heads a group somewhat like an audience, but workshops are not just run-of-the-mill speech situations; they have an immediacy about them that gives one a vision of eager people rolling up their sleeves and hurrying to the shop to get right down to work.

The workshop leader needs to know about the participants in order to prepare a workshop that targets their needs and expectations. Following is an example of a workshop that illustrates what you, as leader, should do and think about before getting to work on your workshop game plan. The workshop leader in this example is the president of a small, successful advertising agency. She has been invited by a local professional business organization to run a workshop aimed at helping its members promote new business activity on a limited budget.

WORKSHOP LEADER CHECKLIST

Drawing on guidelines similar to those used by a guest speaker, this workshop leader goes through the appropriate checklist to find the answers that will help her develop an appropriate plan of action for the workshop.

1. How many people will be in the group?
   The answer to this question will help the leader determine what kind of participant involvement is possible. Should she consider dividing the group into small core groups, or have them work on projects individually?

Formidable Formats: Workshops, Seminars, Panels • 189

2. In what kind of businesses are the attendees engaged?
   This information will help the leader determine what problems, examples, case histories, and other elements would be most meaningful to the participants.
3. What are the demographics of the participant group? What is their age? Sex? Education? What are their special interests? Problems?
   This will tell the leader what kind of people she will be working with.
4. How do these business people usually promote their businesses? Do they use radio, television, newspapers, magazines, flyers, or any other means?
   This answer will help the workshop leader focus on information these people should know about.
5. What problems do participants currently have regarding business promotion?
   The answer to this question could be the substance of the workshop.

After the workshop leader in this example mulled over the answers she got, she decided to do her workshop on "How to Prepare a New Business Promotion Letter."

A workshop requires a two-part game plan: the presentation of the how-to material and then the participation segment. Our workshop leader mapped out her game plan just as you would map out a speech. (See her speech statement below.) First, she outlined her entire approach and gathered her visual aids and handouts. This workshop leader has had a great deal of experience speaking before large and small audiences, and always plans her presentations with care and attention to all details, big and small. She feels that when the speaker has the extra responsibility of actually teaching a task, on top of the routine explanation, each element has to be tested, timed, handled, and rehearsed. She's right. So she rehearsed her total workshop game plan, referring to her script (presentation outline) and running the overhead projector, so that she could practice reviewing her examples and plan how best to show them and then remove them smoothly when she finished focusing on them. She did all of this in a stand-up dress rehearsal that included conscious control of presentation body language essentials as well as all of the other elements in the workshop. The reason she goes through all of this, beyond the obvious need to be prepared, is that it makes her feel better and makes her better able to handle her nervousness. Rehearsal is invaluable!

Here's how our ad agency president plotted her two-part workshop game plan using the Snyder Four-Card System:

PRESENTATION SEGMENT

>Speech Statement: How to write a new business promotion letter.

>Audience: Professional business organization members.

>Pattern: Chronological.

Introduction: Use a letter to promote new business.

>Background: The success I've had in advertising agency business using promotion by letter to attract new business.

Body: How to write a new business letter.

>Step 1. Examples of successful letters.

>Step 2. Case histories showing other successful letters that attracted new business to service and product businesses, using different approaches to achieve the same end.

>Step 3. Examples of putting it all together—unusual approaches, twists, gimmicks—using an audience member's business in a dynamic on-the-spot workup of a good letter.

Conclusion: Recap the essentials of steps 1, 2, and 3.

PARTICIPATION SEGMENT

1. Task assignment explanation—list what you (a workshop member) have to sell and its benefits.
2. Task exercise—write a letter promoting your unique offering to a specific prospect whose business you want.
3. Task evaluation—group/leader feedback and critique of participants' samples written during Exercise 2.

A workshop emphasizes the exchange of ideas. It involves the group members. In most workshops the leader demonstrates the application of techniques or skills, and then the participants try out the process themselves.

PANELS

Panels are popular, and for good reasons: They're efficient (if run right), and the audience gets to hear different speakers (three or four works best) and different points of view on a subject of interest—all in one program package. A lot of hard information can be shared quickly in the kind of spirited, short exchanges that panels encourage; the interaction possibilities of panelist with panelist, moderator with panelist, audience with panelists, and panelists with audience can add up to a stimulating, informative experience.

If you're planning to set up a panel program, you can go the traditional route, invent a new kind of panel, or crossbreed existing panel types. Use your imagination. This invention idea is equally applicable to meetings, seminars, workshops, and so forth; don't be limited by what's been done. But panels, like other types of speech situations, take planning. You can and should use the Snyder Four-Card System in thinking through your panel program—from analyzing your audience to deciding on your panel's subject and then focusing on a single area for each panelist to concentrate upon. You will help your panelists if you give them their speech statements when you extend the invitation to be on the panel. (Make sure the speech statement takes into account the panelist's area of expertise on your broad subject.) Then all will know what they are responsible for, overlapping will be minimized, and the panel audience will reap the rewards of your preparation. When you know exactly what type of panel you will have, based on the speech statements, you can move on to the panel design (introduction, body, conclusion), just as you would in developing a speech.

To moderate a panel successfully you have to know what

you're doing, take nothing personally, and maintain a cool control. The moderator must have more than a passing knowledge of group dynamics, and should know how to interact and solve problems on the spot. A good moderator has to orchestrate the entire event *without being the center of attention* by guiding the proceedings, restraining the long-winded, and quelling the argumentative, and by bringing the program to a conclusion at just the right moment, when it is still in high gear, not when it has run out of steam. A good moderator should have a theatrical sense and be dedicated to the success of the program. Preparation is always a main ingredient in any success story.

Being a Panelist

Moderating a panel is one thing; being a panel member is quite another. If you are asked to be a member of a panel, be sure to find out how large the panel will be. If you are fortunate, there will not be more than two or three other panelists, but the only way to avoid being an echo of the other panel members is to ask your contact person some pertinent questions.

Checklist for Panel Speakers

1. What particular aspect of the topic do you want me to focus on?
2. How long would you like me to speak?
3. Would you tell me about the audience that will attend?
4. Will the questions and answers follow each panelist or after all the panelists have spoken?
5. Who are the other panelists?
6. What is each one going to focus on?
7. Will we be getting together before the program to discuss our parts?
8. May I have the names and phone numbers of the other panelists?

9. Who will coordinate the panelists and introduce us? May I have that person's name and address, so that I can send my biography to her in advance?
10. Where will the panel be held? Time? Place? Date?

Putting Together a Panel—Tips for the Host/Contact

When you're planning a panel program—whether for a business, social, political, religious, educational, activist, or any other audience—prepare! Prepare it all down to the last detail. Your audience expects you to deliver a professional event; they will give you their time, and you make sure that you are giving them the gift they're coming to hear: a well-packaged, audience-related panel program.

The following hypothetical example describes a panel program that had all the earmarks of success, that could have been a memorable evening, but failed due to lack of preparation. The program was sponsored by an organization of five hundred members. Two hundred came to this program, because the three panelists had great appeal to this segment of the membership. But this could be any organization—it could be one you belong to. See if some of the things that happened in this event are reminiscent of promising evenings you've witnessed that did not fulfill their potential.

Among the things that happened that should not have happened was that when the host began, the audience immediately sensed her lack of preparation and direction, and they resented it. As moderator, she did not adequately introduce the panelists—that is, she told the audience nothing about the individuals beyond their names, which she did not say clearly enough to be understood.

When the host had originally invited the guests, she had not asked them to prepare their remarks or presentations, so they didn't. They winged it. Two of the three speakers rambled on and on, not knowing exactly what to say. Only one panelist knew what to do. She was a natural impromptu speaker with a sense of humor and a sense of the audience's expectations. She alone was a peak in that evening's valley of boredom.

The host/moderator did ask each panelist questions, but unfortunately, the questions were not thought through. They were uninteresting to the audience, and, worse, the answers to them were obvious; the audience knew the answers before the panelists responded. Many of the questions posed by the host were answered with a simple yes or no, and she let them die with that.

The final section of the evening was devoted to an exchange between the audience and the panelists—a Question and Answer period. Sounds fine, but it wasn't, because the moderator lost control and a few things went awry that should not have. Some of the questions were long speeches, and boring, rambling ones, at that; the panelists went off on tangents that were indiscreet and in poor taste (which caused a certain amount of audience discomfort); and the moderator was not listening carefully enough to anticipate and control the obvious turn the audience's questions were taking. The evening was a disaster.

If you're responsible for pulling together a panel program, you've got to do the job from beginning to end. There are no shortcuts. The example just given paints a picture of unprepared failure, but that needn't happen to you. The simple formula for moderator success is to prepare an outline that sketches out exactly what kind of program you want. Then write the guidelines you'll have to follow to achieve your end. For example:

1. Put your program on paper. Think it over; brainstorm.
    a. What's it going to be about?
    b. Use the same process you would to focus on a speech; what's the single subject your panel will discuss?
    c. Clarify in your own mind what your purpose is.
    d. Formulate a speech statement—then you'll be ready to move on.
    e. Decide on speakers to invite who have expertise in the area your speech statement has pinpointed.
    f. Decide what you're going to ask each one of your panelists to talk about. Write a speech statement to give to

each one of them, so that they will know what you want them to talk about and you won't end up with ramblers or echos.

2. Make a list of the program points that the panelists must know.

   a. Your audience.

   b. A detailed panel game plan.

3. Make a list of what you have to do for the program itself.

   a. Prepare your own presentation/introduction—make it short. It should tell your audience briefly about the program, how it will be run, how long it will last.

   b. Prepare concise biographical introductions for each panelist. Rehearse all of the above, so that you can say it, not read it.

   c. Prepare questions you might ask the panelists after each presentation. Prepare a name tag for each panelist.

4. And during the program don't forget what your job is.

   a. Make your audience feel you are in control. Welcome them enthusiastically.

   b. Give your guests the red carpet treatment when you introduce them. Say each panelist's name clearly.

   c. Listen when your panelists are speaking, so that you can frame intelligent, probing audience-tilted questions.

   d. Time your speakers. Make up a simple 3 x 5 card that says "Time's up!" Tell each panelist you will flash it at five minutes and would appreciate it if they concluded right after they notice it.

   e. After each speaker finishes, you should immediately rise and take the reins, so that your audience will be carried along with the momentum (ask your prepared questions, move along, introduce the next panelist and so on).

   f. If a panelist answers a question with a simple yes, probe for more details. Ask "How?" "What else can you tell us?" "What happened then?"

   g. Conclude on time. Invite people with unanswered questions, or those too shy to ask questions in public, to come up to the platform to talk to the panelists.

h. Summarize the highlights of the program so that people have a few key things to think about when they go home.

i. Generously thank your panelists and bid everyone adieu.

19

SPEAKER'S SMORGASBORD: ANSWERS TO A VARIETY OF CONCERNS

MICROPHONES

There are hundreds of different microphones. They come in all shapes and sizes, and are made for different uses, ranging from the mikes used at lecterns to mikes used on radio and television.

When speaking before a large audience, you should always ask for the use of a microphone. It will make your speaking job a lot easier. The best advice I can give you about microphones is this: Let them do the job of carrying your conversational voice to all corners of the room or hall with no strain on you. A mike is an aid, a friend. Don't be in awe of it; don't be afraid of it. Just use it and be glad your voice doesn't have to work its way to the last row of the auditorium on its own.

The best way to handle a microphone is to find out how it works by either asking the sound technician (if there is one) or by observing how it works for other people. While you are being introduced by the host, observe how far the host stands back from the mike and how far the head of the mike is from the host's chin. Notice, too, how much volume the host is putting behind his or her voice. Then, when you arrive at the lectern, you can follow your host's example. But remember that when you arrive at the lectern, you will have to make the necessary microphone adjustments based on your needs and your height—if you are five feet five inches and the host is six feet two, tilt the microphone down, for example.

If the mike is a stationary one (such as a floor mike or gooseneck mike attached to the speaker's stand), you'll have to stay behind it during your entire presentation. The microphone must always be between you and your audience. If you move away from the mike, or if you move your head to the left or to the right, your audience will not hear what you are saying. If you remember to look out across a stationary mike as you speak, you will always be heard. And whatever you do, do not refer to, joke about, or become flustered over the presence of a mike. Say nothing about it; just use it as if you were an old pro!

Another microphone type you might have occasion to use is the chest or lavaliere mike. This type is hung around your neck with a wire left trailing behind you. Two considerations to keep in mind regarding a lavaliere are: 1) Be careful not to trip on the wire, and 2) don't touch the microphone. Hands off. Ignore it. Speak in your normal, natural tone of voice—conversationally.

The newest type of mike is the button or lapel microphone. It clips on, has little weight and is easy to ignore. Don't touch this one, either. And remember, a microphone is a speaker's friend.

HANDSHAKES

In the business world, a handshake is the first contact you have with a new prospect, colleague, or client. It is also likely to be the only physical contact you will have with that person. What happens between the two of you at that moment of contact can influence the success of your association. A handshake opens the business transaction. It talks. It sends a message to each receiver. A good handshake is an invaluable asset that communicates warmth, concern, genuine pleasure —all positive signals. Unfortunately, an unsuccessful handshake can harm you by communicating weakness, disinterest, indifference—all negative signals.

How do you execute a handshake that sends the receiver a positive message? A handshake should be firm. The degree of firmness, of course, is up to you, but very firm is better than fairly firm. Take the other person's hand in yours and envelop it with a full, deep grip. Hold it long enough for a signal of concern to register with the receiver, and while you're shaking hands establish eye contact to reaffirm your interest in meeting the person.

Women who feel these guidelines are not feminine should reconsider. Test your theory. Ask a friend which handshake of yours she prefers, which one says the best things about you and about her—the limp, passive one or the firm, frank one just detailed? Remember, a handshake communicates the first message to someone who does not know you. Even after you get to know people, your handshake reinforces their impression of you. When you shake hands, say something positive. After all, it's body language.

DRY MOUTH

If your mouth tends to feel dry and uncomfortable when you speak in front of an audience for an extended period of time, here are a few remedies you might try. Drink water. Stress and dehydration go together. Moisten your mouth by taking sips of water during your presentation delivery. If you know that you tend to get speaker's dry mouth and will need to drink water at the lectern, be sure to order a pitcher of water and glass in advance, and, by all means, rehearse your speech at home pausing to take water, so that you will be able to execute this seemingly simple activity in front of your audience without awkwardness.

If you can induce yawning prior to speaking, or before you are introduced, do so. Yawning lubricates the mouth. Try it, but not in front of your audience.

Another simple and surprisingly successful method of handling dry mouth is putting a dab of Vaseline on the inner part of your lower lip. This also keeps the mouth moist.

If you are able to psych yourself with mind-over-matter exercises, try this one. Picture a plump, yellow lemon about to be cut into by a sharp knife. If you imagined that and were able to induce salivation by self-suggestion, you might use this technique to water your dry mouth.

Avoid antihistamines and aspirin. They dry the throat.

Avoid large amounts of Vitamin C. This vitamin can dry your vocal cords.

Smoking dries the throat and constricts blood vessels.

Reduce stress. Go back to Chapter 9 to review how. Find a way to handle nervousness, so that you can minimize dehydration and dry mouth.

HUMOR

If you can make another human being or a whole audience smile, chuckle, chortle, titter, laugh, or guffaw, do it. But don't use jokes. Use humor. Your own sense of humor. As a rule, jokes do not fit the average person's presentation needs as well as your natural sense of humor.

The fact is, very few people can handle somebody else's jokes and make them work. Jokes have to be stretched, cut, and reshaped to come close to being germane to a particular speech subject. Usually, they do not do the job; they just distract the audience. So don't use jokes. Do use your own sense of humor as it flows naturally out of and with your speech's message.

LISTENING

A good listener is a good speaker, because listening is the best way to improve your language. That's how we learn to speak in the first place. Unfortunately, few of us really learn how to listen. Listening takes energy. It requires the sifting and sorting of information. It involves the use of the senses. It demands being aware of the emotions between the lines. A good listener is valued. And when we as speakers are listened to, we feel good. A speaker wants to be listened to, especially after having gone to all the trouble to put together a thoughtful speech.

There are three basic steps involved in listening. The first is hearing. You have to hear the ideas in order to absorb information, and that's work. Your thoughts are racing along at a clip of about 400 to 500 words per minute whereas the speaker's pace is only between 125 to 160 words per minute. To listen effectively, you've got to pull back, slow down, and pay close attention to what is being said. Listen with affection; it will help you hear. The second step is understanding. As you listen, ask yourself, "What is this person trying to tell me?" Be curious. Show interest. Your conscious body language will gear you up to understand as you listen. Give the speaker body language cues: eye contact, nods, smiles, concentrating silence. When appropriate, give verbal cues to encourage the speaker, as well as to indicate you do understand—such as "Oh," "Hmm," or "I see." The third step is remembering. What was said? Thus, the acronym for better listening is HUR: hearing, understanding, remembering. Train yourself to isolate the central idea, the key point the speaker is trying to make. Then hang on to it. To make sure you have the key point, restate it to yourself or to the person who is speaking to you. Or ask the speaker a question about it. A good listener's mind is open. It says "tell me more." A good speaker should believe that the listener's mind is always asking, "Of what use is this to me?" Good communication and good listening will result if both speaker and listener keep these thoughts in mind.

HANDOUTS

Do you need handouts? That's the first question you have to ask yourself when you jump to the conclusion, "I'll use a handout!" Handouts can be excellent additions to your postspeech success. Notice that I said *post*speech. Promise handouts when you refer to them during your presentation, but don't hand them out until after your speech. Handouts should never be given out before your presentation, because handouts cause people's attention to be riveted on the handout instead of on you. Only on rare occasions, when your audience for some reason must have your handout in their hands, would you distribute it before or during your speech. In that case, distribute it only at the exact moment they must have it, not before. If you were going to demonstrate to a small audience how to eat with chopsticks, for instance, they would need to have the chopsticks in hand at a given moment in your presentation.

Handouts can be useful and influential if used thoughtfully. They are generally inexpensive. They might provide your listeners with summary material to refer to in the future. They can include visuals—drawings, pictures, charts— that your listeners might want to keep. And a handout has value for those who were unable to attend on the day of your presentation; attentive members of your audience can take them along for their absent colleagues.

Consider these points about handouts: If you think the handout you're considering is just fluff, and will be tossed out by the recipient as soon as a round file comes into view, don't bother. The same holds true if you don't have the time or budget to prepare a professional-looking handout. Don't bother.

You can refer to your handout within your presentation, and tell people that they can have a copy and where they can pick it up after you are finished. If the handout contains a chart you are speaking about, project it in your presentation on an overhead or slide projector, and promise the audience a copy of it—later.

A good handout is carefully considered, respectfully handled, generously promised, and prominently available. Be sure to put your name, title, company, and the date on each handout. It will help the recipient remember where he got it six months down the road. And title it; you can use your speech statement as your title, after you've reworked it into a catchy phrase.

HANDLING HECKLERS

If you are harassed by a heckler with impertinent questions, gibes, or badgering, you've got to do something about it. The audience will expect you to handle it. Don't disappoint them. Keep cool, and remember Snyder's Law. Naturally every situation is different. The following suggestions should give you some ideas, some ammunition, for subduing hecklers. In an actual situation, of course, you would need to rely on your own good judgment.

1. When you know you are faced with a heckler, make sure your body language says, "You can't get to me." Project a cool, collected, in-control message through your posture and facial expression.

2. Diffuse a heckler's anger with your sense of humor. George Bernard Shaw handled a disagreeable heckler with this remark: "I quite agree with you, my friend, but who are you and I against so many?"

3. Invite the heckler to see you afterward since there is not enough time to go into details at the moment.

4. Suggest that your heckler seek out an authoritative source: "The answer you're looking for is superbly explained in So and So's book,————. It's all there. Check it out. It's just too long to go into here."

5. If your heckler continually tries to impose his opinion on you, avoid recognizing him by keeping your eye contact elsewhere. Ignore him. If he demands attention, tell him you first want to give others a chance to be heard.

6. Don't get into a lengthy exchange or a shouting match with a heckler. Always handle your heckler with dispatch —and move on briskly and coolly.

7. If you are thoroughly prepared and rehearsed, know your audience and your facts, you have nothing to worry about. Using good sense, tact, and humor, you'll be more than a match for any heckler.

20
BRAVO!
BRAVA!

And now, for a few final words in this long memo from me to you—some things to think about now that you've reached the end of your journey through this book. And for those of you who want one more shot in the arm, here is my message to you for the last time—in miniature.

Imagine you are sitting on a stage before an audience to which you are about to be introduced. You sit erect in your chair. Tall. Confident. Presidential.

You psych yourself. You know what you're doing. Your speech is well prepared, well rehearsed.

You have the tools; you know the techniques involved in public speaking. You have nothing to worry about.

You're being introduced now. Your biography is being said. You listen objectively. It sounds fine. It should. You wrote it. The audience is impressed with your credentials, interested in you, the confident figure before them, and interested in what you plan to talk about.

You're ready. You know who they are, why they're there, and how to reach them and hold them.

The host's introduction is over. All eyes are on you as you rise and move to the lectern, confident in the knowledge that your body language speaks silently but positively about you.

206 • SPEAK FOR YOURSELF WITH CONFIDENCE

At the lectern you feel a little heady, but that's positive nervousness—channeled energy. It's that excitement, that zesty exhilaration a presenter must have, and you welcome it.

You adjust your delivery notes, stand solidly on both feet, take a relaxing breath or two, acclimate yourself. In that fleeting pause before you speak, you create a moment of contact with your audience. You do it with your eyes.

Will you go directly into your attention-getting introduction with a friendly smile—if, in fact, a smile is appropriate—or will you use some other fitting facial expression?

Whatever you do, you will use knowledge and good taste, knowing what is right and, more important, what works.

Your strong, positive opening makes the audience feel good. They know they are in capable hands.

First you tell them what you're going to tell them, then you tell them what you just promised to tell them, and finally you tell them what you told them.

As you speak, you articulate well. They don't strain to hear you. You don't apologize. You don't resort to verbal crutches. You sound great.

You move along in your speech, captivating your audience with your carefully thought-out, researched, rehearsed, structured speech.

Your eyes sweep the audience, letting them know you are looking into their eyes, into their souls.

Your speech is simple. Conversational. Concrete. Localized. Prepared for the ear. For their ears.

It has been wrought and chiseled to communicate effectively, and it does.

It gives each person in the audience a gift. A small gem of knowledge. It teaches. It enlightens.

You deliver your presentation with authority. Your body language and your voice are in concert.

Your audience grasps the subject and the purpose, and they are moved, just as you planned.

They applaud appreciatively.

And so they should; you've learned your lessons well.

Bravo! Brava!

SUGGESTED FURTHER READING

The Speech Writing Guide, by James J. Welsch (John Wiley & Sons).

Speaking Up, by Janet Stone and Jane Bachner (McGraw-Hill).

Speech Can Change Your Life, by Dorothy Sarnoff (Dell).

Speech Communication, by Raymond S. Ross (Prentice-Hall).

Image Impact, edited by Jacqueline Thompson (A & W Publishers).

Effective Business and Technical Presentations, by George L. Morrisey (Addison-Wesley).

Functional Business Presentations, by Paul R. Timm (Prentice-Hall).

Language and Woman's Place, by Robin Lakoff (Harper Colophon Books).

Body Politics, by Nancy Henley (Prentice-Hall).

How to Hold a Better Meeting, by Frank Snell (Cornerstone Library).

The Quotable Woman, edited and compiled by Elaine Partnow (Anchor Press/Doubleday).

How to Develop Self-Confidence and Influence People by Public Speaking, by Dale Carnegie (Pocket Books).

INDEX

Accent, 104–105
Acronyms, 104–105
Age, of audience, 5–6
Alliteration, 50–52
Allusion, 50–52
Anecdote, 45–46
Antidotes to nervousness, 109–116
Antithesis, 52–54
Arousing curiosity, 35–38. *See also* Mind grabbers
Audience, 1–2, 57–58
  and subject selection, 14–19
  TV, 163–164
  what you should know about, 5–13

Bar chart, 84–87
Bartlett's Familiar Quotations, 37–38
Biography, 119–123

Body language, 92–99
  and meetings, 175–176
  in question and answer sessions, 133
  rehearsing, 102–104
  and TV appearances, 159–162, 164–168
Body of speech
  card, 37–39
  developing, 45–56, 61–66
Breath control, 106–107

Carter, Jimmy, 161–164
Case histories, 46–48
Cause/effect pattern, 28–29
Chalk boards, 80–83
Charts, 80–83
Chronological pattern, 26–27
Churchill, Winston, 76–77
Clothes, 106–107
Comparisons, 46–48

210 • Index

Conclusion, 64–66, 104–105
  card, 42–44
Contact person, 7–8
Cue cards, 73–75
Curve chart, 85–87

Definitions, 48–50
Delivery
  day, 106–107
  methods, 67–70
  systems, 68–75
Demonstrations, 46–50, 85–87
Description, 48–50
Detailed outline, 70–72
Diction, 104–107
Displaying Objects, 85–87
Dominant purpose, *see* Purpose
Dramatic events, 12–13
Drawing figures, 80–83
Dry mouth, 198–200

Education level, of audience, 7–8
Enthusiasm, 67–68
Examples, 46–48
Extemporaneous speech, 68–70
Eye contact, 67–68, 97–99
  as feedback, 97–99
  rehearsing, 104–105
  and TV appearances, 163–164

Facial expression, and TV appearances, 161–166

Fear, 108–116. *See also* Nervousness
  cures for, 111–115
Featured speaker, 7–13
  biography of, 119–123
  checklist, 7–10
  introducing, 117–123
Figures of speech, 50–56
Film, 90–91
Flannel boards, 77–83
Flip charts, 74–75
Focus, narrowing, 24–25
Foreign words and phrases, 104–107
Full text system, 70–72

Garroway, Dave, 168–170
Good Advice (Safire), 37–38
Graphs, 85–87

Handouts, 48–50, 200–204
Hands, what to do with, 95–97
Handshakes, 198–200
Hecklers, 202–204
Humor, 200–202
Hyperbole, 52–54

Impromptu speech, 68–70, 134–142
  preparing, 135–142
Interviewing, on TV, 170–174
Introducing the speaker, 117–126
Introduction, 58–60, 104–105
  card, 33–38
  devices, 33–38

Index • 211

James, William, 112–113

Kennedy, John F., 52–54
King, Martin Luther, Jr., 76–77
Know-your-audience checklist, 5–6, 9–10

Language, 3. *See also* Diction
Lincoln, Abraham, 76–77
Line chart, 85–87
Listening, 200–202
Loaded questions, 129–132

Main points, 39–42
  building on, 37–39, 45–46, 60–66
Makeup, for TV appearances, 164–166
Manuscript, 70–72, 74–75
Meetings, 175–186
  briefings, 183–186
  creative, 181–185
  leading, 176–178
  problem-solving, 180–183
  staff, 178–181
  training, 183–185
Memorization, 67–70
Mental picture system, 73–74
Metaphors, 50–52
Microphones, 9–10, 197–200
  boom, 164–166
  clip-on, 164–166, 198–200
  lavaliere, 164–166, 197–198
  table-top, 164–166
Mind grabbers, 9–13
  for TV appearances, 163–164, 165–166

Moderator, 192–193, 194–196
Motions, 178–181
Murrow, Edward R., 33–34

Narrative, 45–46. *See also* Anecdotes
Nervousness, 1–2, 9–10, 108–116. *See also* Dry mouth; Fear
  positive, 113–116
Newly coined words, 200–202

Occupations, of audience, 7–8
Onomatopoeia, 52–54
Opinions, 48–50
Outline
  detailed, 70–72
  skeleton, 70–72
Overhead projections, 50, 74, 89–91
Oxymoron, 52–54

Panelist, 192–193
Panels, 190–193
Parallelism, 52–54
Patterns to model speech on, 26–30, 31–32
  cause/effect, 28–29
  chronological, 26–27
  problem/solution, 28–29
  spatial (space description), 29–30
  topical, 26–29
Personal experience, 45–49
Personification, 50–52
Picture system, 73–74
Pie chart, 80–84

Pre-interviews, for TV appearances, 164–166
Presentation, 64–65. *See also* Delivery
Problem/solution pattern, 28–30
Promotions, 163–166
Proper nouns, 104–105
Props, 85–87
Purpose
  deciding on dominant, 17–23, 58–60
  five basic, 20–23
  and TV appearances, 131–132

Question
  in introduction, 33–36
  rhetorical, 52–54
Question and answer period, 124–133
  dealing with loaded questions in, 129–132
  rehearsing for, 102–104
Quotable Woman, The, 37–38
Quotations, 48–50
  as introductory device, 37–38

Radio appearances, 159–160, 170–174
Reading speech, 68–70
Rehearsal, 100–107
  for TV appearances, 161–162
Repetition, 48–50
Restatement, 48–50

Rhetorical questions, 52–54
Robert's Rules of Order, 180–181

Safire, William, 37–38
SEE factor, 67–68
  and TV appearances, 166–168
Seminars, 187–188
Sex
  of audience, 5–6
  as topic, 10–12
Shaw, George Bernard, 202–204
Similes, 50–52
Skeleton outline system, 70–72
Slides, 74–75, 88–89
Snyder four-card system, 31–44, 54–56
  and impromptu speaking, 168–170
  and radio and TV appearances, 159–160
Social and economic background, of audience, 7–8
Sorensen, Ted, 52–54
Spatial (space description) pattern, 28–29
Special interest of audience, using, for introduction, 35–36
Speech purposes, 20–23
  to amuse, 22–23
  to convince, 20–22
  to impress, 20–23
  to inform, 20–22
  to move the audience to action, 22–23

Speech samples, 143–158
Speech specifics, 45–56
Speech statement, 58–60
 card, 31–34
 formulating, 14–25
Speech timing, 102–104
Spontaneity, 67–68
Spotlight,
 and visual aids, 76–80
Stacking and linking, 73–74
Startling statements, 35–36
Statistics, 46–48
Stories and anecdotes, 35–36
 See also Anecdotes;
 Narratives
Structure notes system, 70–74
Subject, 57–58
 selecting single, 14–19
 specific, 24–25, 57–60
Subject Areas—Mind Grabbers, 9–15

Tape, 90–91
Television, 159–172
Topical pattern, 26–29
Transitions, 48–52
Twain, Mark, 137–139, 175–176
Two-L position, 93–95

Visual aids, 46–50, 76–91
 direct, 77–87
 dynamic, 90–91
 as introductory device, 35–36
 projected, 85–91
 rehearsing, 77–80, 102–104
 timing of, 77–80
 types of, 77–91

Word chart, 77–80
Workshops, 187–191

More MENTOR and SIGNET Reference Books

(0451)

- [ ] **ALL ABOUT WORDS by Maxwell Numberg and Morris Rosenblum.** Two language experts call on history, folklore, and anecdotes to explain the origin, development, and meaning of words. (624947—$4.50)*

- [ ] **WORDS FROM THE MYTHS by Isaac Asimov.** A fascinating exploration of our living heritage from the ancient world. Isaac Asimov retells the ancient stories—from Chaos to the siege of Troy—and describes their influence on modern language . . . and modern life. (123778—$1.95)

- [ ] **INSTANT WORD POWER by Norman Lewis.** A fast, effective way to build a rich and dynamic vocabulary. Entertaining exercises and challenging self-tests enable the student to master hundreds of new words and polish spelling and grammar skills. (117913—$3.50)

- [ ] **MASTERING SPEED READING by Norman C. Maberly.** Basic steps and drills with illustrations, charts and tests provide self-instruction in speed reading. (098579—$1.75)*

*Prices slightly higher in Canada

Buy them at your local bookstore or use this convenient coupon for ordering.

NEW AMERICAN LIBRARY,
P.O. Box 999, Bergenfield, New Jersey 07621

Please send me the books I have checked above. I am enclosing $_____
(please add $1.00 to this order to cover postage and handling). Send check or money order—no cash or C.O.D.'s. Prices and numbers are subject to change without notice.

Name_____

Address_____

City_____State_____Zip Code_____

Allow 4-6 weeks for delivery.
This offer is subject to withdrawal without notice.